More praise for
*The Seven Dumbest Relationship Mistakes
Smart People Make*

"Insightful . . . Once you start turning the pages, this book can either: 1) make you angry because you feel you've been 'found out'; or 2) prompt a smile as you quietly identify with a category or two. . . . [Bushong's] categories aren't pithy. They are solid guides for contemplation for people who want to learn and grow. . . . This is an honest book."
—*The Rocky Mountain News*

"[Bushong] addresses herself directly to women in relationships with men, treating her readership as strong, smart and competent, and shows them how to balance taking and giving."
—*Publishers Weekly*

"Clearly written . . . A no-frills guide to keeping relationships honest."
—*Library Journal*

"I was immediately hooked."
—*Milwaukee Journal-Sentinel*

# THE
# SEVEN DUMBEST
# RELATIONSHIP
# MISTAKES
# SMART PEOPLE
# MAKE

# THE
# SEVEN DUMBEST
# RELATIONSHIP
# MISTAKES
# SMART PEOPLE
# MAKE

## CAROLYN N. BUSHONG, L.P.C.

Fawcett Books
The Random House Publishing Group • New York

A Fawcett Book
Published by The Random House Publishing Group

Copyright © 1997 by Carolyn N. Bushong, L.P.C.

www.ballantinebooks.com

Library of Congress Catalog Card Number: 98-96965

ISBN: 0-449-00569-0

This edition published by arrangement with Villard Books, a division of Random House, Inc.

Text design by Oksana Kushnir

Manufactured in the United States of America

First Ballantine Books Edition: April 1999

7  9  10  8  6

To Alan,
the love of my life

# ACKNOWLEDGMENTS

Most of all I want to thank my loving mate, Alan, who, after nine years, is still by my side, stronger and more supportive than ever. We met after I had made most of the seven mistakes (and he had, too), and we were both eager to change and grow healthy together. I appreciate how this man who has prided himself on being "discreet" has handled my discussing our lives on TV and radio, and in this book. I also greatly appreciate Alan's ability to continue his loving support while I was often preoccupied with this project.

I also want to thank my family, who spent our recent vacations together watching me sit at the computer. I also thank them for resolving issues with me and allowing me to work through my past with them so I could stop making these mistakes permanently. I especially thank my sister, Ruth Krueger, who is also a therapist and has become my best friend. I also want to thank my nephew Brett and Alan's daughter Alecia for understanding and knowing how much I loved them even when we weren't able to talk for months at a time.

Special thanks to Patty Romanowski for her guidance and way with words. She earned her pseudo-degree in counseling as she helped me bring this book to fruition with her talent, dedication, and unbelievable understanding of the subject.

Special thanks to Suzanne Wickham-Beaird at Villard Books for seeing the potential of this book. It was her ability to match my knowledge with what she knows women want that brought the book to focus.

And thanks to Debi Galbaugh, who never flinched when I sent her the next revision to put on the computer—over and over again. Her unfailing persistence and dedication is very much appreciated.

And thanks to Dr. Ida Truscott, who has consulted with me over the years and was always there to help me clarify and sort my ideas, and Dr. Virginia Moore, my first mentor, whose enthusiasm in the field kept me focused.

And thanks to my agent, Alan Nevins, who reassured me each time I panicked.

And thanks to television producers Scott Martin and Donna Wright for their savvy media direction. I have valued their professional association dearly. Thanks to John Peake, who gave me free rein in developing my own radio show, to Rick O'Bryan, my great *Passion Phones* cohost, and to my attorney Michael London for his superb negotiation skills. Thanks also to magazine editors Bonnie Krueger of *Complete Woman,* Stephanie von Hirschberg of *New Woman,* Diane Baroni of *Cosmopolitan,* Catherine Romano of *Marie Claire,* and Adelaide Farah of *Woman's Own* for regularly seeking my expertise.

And thanks to all my clients—those whose stories led to this book, those who are in it, and especially those who broadened and deepened my understanding of these seven mistakes. It's extremely satisfying to watch my clients change and grow and gain control of their lives and their relationships.

# CONTENTS

Acknowledgments                                              ix
Introduction                                                xiii

**Part One: Why Smart People Make Dumb Mistakes**
  1. How Relationships Really Work                   3
  2. Relationships 101: Why We Do the Things
    We Do                                  24

**Part Two: The Seven Dumbest Mistakes: How to Stop
Making Them**
  3. Mistake Number One: Forcing Intimacy           49
  4. Mistake Number Two: Expecting Your Mate
    to Read Your Mind                       75
  5. Mistake Number Three: Playing the Martyr       104
  6. Mistake Number Four: Thinking You Are
    Always Right                           129
  7. Mistake Number Five: Rescuing Your Mate        152
  8. Mistake Number Six: Taking Your Mate
    for Granted                            177
  9. Mistake Number Seven: Letting Passion Die      200

  Epilogue                                         227

# INTRODUCTION

"I have a failed marriage and, before that, a failed live-in relationship," Sally, a forty-eight-year-old businesswoman tells me. "And every time I think I've found the right person, I try so hard—he never seems to appreciate it, and then the relationship dies. Now I'm in love with someone, but I'm afraid I'm going to make the same mistakes again."

"I thought he was perfect, so I slept with him on the second date," thirty-four-year-old Angela says. "I know we were meant for each other, but he's never called me again. Why are men so afraid to commit?"

"He says that he loves me, and I've never felt so close to anyone else in my life," Karen, a late-twenty-something lawyer says. "So why can't he be there for me when I'm upset? He just doesn't seem to understand how I feel. Why do I always have to spell it out for him? He makes it so hard."

Like most of my clients—indeed, like most people—these women are all wondering, *Why can't I find the right relationship?* Or *Why can't I make a relationship work?* To many, a good relationship seems an impossible dream, whereas bad ones are like recurring nightmares. Most of the women I've spoken with sincerely want to change and improve their love life, but everything they know about love—from what they, as children, witnessed between their parents to their girlfriends' well-meaning advice—tells them that to love is to be hurt, that the healthy, esteem-building relationship they dream of is impossible. No wonder they find themselves trapped between contradictory beliefs. If they are single, they tenaciously clutch the fragile hope of finding true love but are convinced their search is doomed. They long for the perfect mate yet secretly believe he does not exist. If they are settled into a relationship, they fervently wish it could be better but believe they must accept less—less love, less sex, less communication, less passion. I'm here to tell you it does not have to be that way.

Most of us believe relationships are difficult because men are immature, we are unworthy, or certain people are just bad. But the real problem with love is that no one ever taught any of us what healthy love is or how to achieve it. As a result, we make one or more of the seven mistakes in love, usually the same one, or several, over and over again. We make most of these mistakes subconsciously, so when we repeat them, we tend to do so without fully realizing what we are doing or why. Because of this, it is important to identify the mistake we are making. Once we determine the mistake (or mistakes) we make, we can then trace the problem to its roots and find effective solutions.

Whenever we make mistakes, we usually make one of the following Seven Dumbest Mistakes:

- We force intimacy.
- We expect our mate to read our mind.
- We play the martyr.
- We assume we are right.
- We rescue our mate.
- We take our mate for granted.
- We let passion die.

So many of us make what I call the Seven Dumbest Mistakes that it's not surprising we regard them and the problems they cause as normal. In truth, they are not normal and in fact result in unhealthy relationships and unhappy people. It doesn't have to be that way.

Both women and men make these mistakes, and both feel victimized by relationships. To be fair, I'd have to say that both actually are victimized. The real tragedy is that so much of the pain I see in my office could have been avoided if only each of us had been taught how to behave in a relationship. Add to that ignorance a generous helping of self-defeating, unrealistic beliefs—*that true love should be easy,* among others—and you have the recipe for disaster. The good news is that the problem is not you or your mate. There are few truly bad people, mostly just bad mistakes and bad scripts that we can't seem to help repeating. And how could it be otherwise? After all, we aren't rewarded for owning up to our mistakes, for setting personal boundaries, for standing up to criticism and manipulation, for resolving issues without creating a winner and a loser.

This book will teach you everything about relationships that no one else taught you. You'll learn how to truly understand your script and then how to rewrite it. I'll show you how to

- recognize and take responsibility for the mistakes you make;
- stop blaming others;
- recognize and change negative behavior patterns;
- establish and protect personal boundaries;
- hold others accountable for the way they treat you;
- avoid staying in relationships for the wrong reasons;
- take charge of your own happiness;
- attract and maintain relationships of integrity.

Women may notice themselves repeating the same patterns from relationship to relationship yet stridently insist that their mate's bad behavior justifies their own or that they "can't help" feeling as they do or that love is just a hurtful game in which disappointment and conflict are the rule, not the exception. Believe me, I've heard it all. I've even been guilty of believing some of these things myself, but I found a better way, and so can you.

## My Own Journey

I have been a practicing psychotherapist for more than twenty years, and in that time I've learned a great deal about men, women, and relationships. I chose the field of relationship counseling for two personal reasons. One was an attempt to "cure" my own parents' marital problems, which I now realize no one could have solved but them; they are now divorced. The second was to lessen my own fear of intimacy, which I have achieved. But it wasn't easy. Over the course of an early three-year marriage, a three-year live-in relationship, and numerous dating relationships, I made every mistake in this book. When men withdrew from me when I tried to *force intimacy,* I was deeply hurt but rationalized my pain by thinking the problem was that they simply were not mature, loving, or giving enough to be there for me. Though I considered myself open, I see now that I often withheld communication because I *expected my lover to read my mind.* When he did not or could not, it was his fault that he failed to see what I needed, not mine. Then I would *play the martyr,* telling anyone who would listen how badly he was mistreating me and how he had failed to make me happy. In some relationships, I overreacted to having been victimized in previous relationships and so would seize control early on, *assuming I was right* about everything. Having been trained as a therapist made me quite adept at blocking my mate's rejection with my "objective" analysis of his problems. Then I would feel a compulsion to solve those problems, so I would try to *rescue my boyfriends* (after all, who knew better than I what was best for them?), then resent them for leaning on me. Anyone who stayed around long enough was soon *taken for granted,* and finally I would become attracted to someone else and *let the passion die.*

   I did not make every mistake in every relationship, and some relationships were better—happier, more fulfilling—than others. But these seven mistakes haunted me. They colored my view of my then current love, and they threatened future relationships, too. Only later did I learn that the real problem encompassed not only the mistake itself but the reasons why I had made it in the first place.

Without realizing it, I was caught in an interminable—but breakable—cycle of disappointment. Through it all, I never believed it was possible to maintain a happy, healthy relationship with a man, much less stay madly in love with, and attracted to, him for any period of time. After all, I had rarely seen anyone else do it. And when I looked at people in the kinds of long-term relationships everyone told me I should want to sacrifice everything for, all I saw were couples who had lost their sparkle, their zest for life. I knew I could never settle for that. And as I became more involved in building my career, it became easier to remain alone. I'd had my fill of wildly passionate, addictive relationships built on equal parts love and hate. They drained me of the energy I needed to focus on my career. I had concluded that all men—or at least the ones I chose—were jerks. I couldn't see the part I had played, the mistakes I had made, the faulty assumptions about men, women, and love that had conspired against my ever finding the love I wanted and deserved.

I was ready to face the rest of my life alone because, I reasoned, it was impossible to have a great relationship with a man. Then I met my current mate, Alan, and he proved me wrong. Now before you assume that Alan came riding into my life on a white steed like a knight in a fairy tale, let me explain. Angry with men and defensive about my part in past relationships, I was not a helpless princess waiting to be rescued. I believed that men were the cause of all relationship problems. And Alan brought a past that included a defunct seventeen-year relationship and his own issues. Yet I could see that Alan was special—a genuinely compassionate man. It wasn't that neither of us had problems; we both had them. The difference this time was that we were both committed to facing them and working them through. So although I have based this book on years of observing and helping thousands of clients—women and men—I have also based it on my own life.

## You Can Stop Making These Dumb Mistakes, Too

Easier said than done, I assure you. But then anything worth doing usually is. The secret that no one bothered to tell you is that you *can* stop making these dumb mistakes. Throughout your life, you've gone through many phases and stages, you've participated in countless relationships, and you've been formed—for better or worse—by these experiences. Parents, other family members, friends, lovers, husbands, even children, might come and go. Your life today may be exactly what it was twenty years ago or totally different from what it was just last week. The sole constant in your life—the one and only thing you can always count on—is you. You are the first person you must understand, listen to, and teach to realize your full potential. Yes, I know, your parents probably were not perfect, previous mates no doubt damaged your self-esteem, and your current love is falling short of your expectations. These are all valid concerns that affect how successfully you deal with issues today. But what about tomorrow? What can you do to loosen the stranglehold of the past, to stop falling into the same self-defeating patterns, to truly live and love life for all it's worth?

## PART ONE

# WHY
# SMART PEOPLE
# MAKE DUMB MISTAKES

# 1

## How Relationships
## Really Work

### The Seven Dumbest Mistakes Smart People Make

First, let's be clear: Relationships were never easy and never will be. We pay lip service to the idea that it takes time and effort to find, nurture, and thrive in a healthy relationship. And, yes, we often make great investments in our relationships only to learn that they were for naught. We then find ourselves amid the wreckage of a love gone wrong, wringing our hands and asking, "Why did he turn out to be such a jerk? What happened to me?" The real question should be, "What could *I* have done to have prevented this?" We often sense that something is wrong, that there is room for improvement, but what exactly we should do and how and why eludes us. Deep down, we fear that we are inadequate and so don't deserve a man to be happy with.

So we vow to turn over a new leaf. We go on a diet, get another degree, change careers, or shop till we drop, trying to make ourselves more attractive to the next Mr. Wonderful. If we're smart, this time we look for someone we believe is completely different, someone who will not treat us as our past lovers did. But not long after we find a new mate, something starts to feel vaguely familiar, and soon the whole relationship assumes a quality of déjà vu. And no wonder: We slip back into making the same mistake again. We may read the self-help books and advice columns, talk to our friends and even a therapist. We may even talk it over with our mate, telling ourselves that if we try harder, say more, promise to change, we will stumble on the hidden key to happiness. When that does not happen and the relationship ends, we replay every conversation, analyzing what happened and sorting out who's right and who's wrong. Maybe we swear we will never go out with someone like "that" again. Maybe we just give up and never fall in love again. However it ends, it is often because—no matter how smart we are—we have repeated one of the Seven Dumbest Mistakes Smart People Make.

---

### Avoid the Seven Dumbest Mistakes
### (Or, Seven Ways to Make Love Really Work)

1. Stop forcing intimacy (and start letting love evolve).
2. Stop expecting your mate to read your mind (and start communicating exactly what you feel and want).
3. Stop playing the martyr (and start refusing to be abused).
4. Stop assuming you are always right (and start opening your mind).
5. Stop rescuing your mate (and control your own life).
6. Stop taking your mate for granted (and start respecting your love).
7. Stop letting passion die (and vow to keep falling in love again and again).

Which of the Seven Dumbest Mistakes have you made in the past? Which do you still make today? If you have trouble choosing only one, relax. Most of us make more than one of these mistakes, and certain common scenarios encompass two or more. Sometimes, making one mistake almost inevitably leads us to make another. For example, when we begin taking our mate for granted, odds are that we will break the bond of sexual attraction and let the passion die sooner or later.

Several factors contribute to our making these mistakes: our past relationships, basic beliefs about people and love, and low self-esteem. We cannot expect to correct our relationship mistakes unless we understand why we make them and—even more important—where we got the ideas that lead us to repeat them. First among our many misunderstandings is our flawed, unrealistic concept of romantic love.

## Our First False Belief: Love Should Be Easy

Where do we get the idea that love should be easy? Everywhere! Poets write of "falling in"—never "working at"—love. Crooners sing of that "magic moment"—not "the daily work of maintaining our love." Yes, relationships are difficult. Yes, they take time and energy, sensitivity and savvy. But they can also be infinitely rewarding and worth nurturing and protecting. To keep any relationship healthy—and especially to keep the love alive—we must accord it the respect and care we would a third person. No matter how closely two people are bonded, their relationship is a separate entity with its own requirements.

When we speak of "men," "women," "relationships," "love," and "marriage," we often fall into the trap of seeing them as predefined entities, monolithic and unchangeable. We talk about what men "should do" and how relationships "should be," but, as I'll discuss later, we rarely consider *why* we think the way we do. More important, until faced with a problem, we don't pay much attention to the consequences. The good news is that regardless of your relationship history or your mate's, your current relationship can be what the two of *you* make of it. Falling in love isn't like moving into one of a million identical, standard-issue high-rise apartments. In fact, nurturing love and protecting love are more like living in a house that you and your mate build, maintain, and sometimes even rebuild over and over again.

I often hear women complaining that their mates "don't listen," "won't change," or "don't really care." Yet when these women are honest, they often find that they never gave their men the chance to prove how much the relationship meant to them. Often women shy away from conflict for fear it will kill the relationship. They may believe it's better to protect their mate than to confront him with problems or that it is nobler to suffer silently than to look like a nag. They may also assume that love is either always easy or always hard or that admitting to problems is a sign of weakness in themselves and in their relationship. Whatever their reasons, these women are embracing ideas that can only undermine love.

People in a healthy relationship responsibly face up to, rather than avoid, the challenges of love. Not only are facing a problem, exploring possible solutions, and improving your relationship essential skills for keeping your house in order, but they also can enhance your self-esteem, your respect for your mate, and your commitment to your relationship. As with any other skill, practice makes perfect. Being able to look back on a successfully resolved issue or a breakthrough in communication gives you an edge the next time your house needs repair.

Good relationships encourage fairness, cooperation, consideration, and respect. Now think of your parents, and ask yourself how many of these values their relationship reflected. If you're like most women with relationship problems, the answer is, Not many, or None.

## Why We Mistake Bad Love for Good

Actions do speak louder than words, and children are particularly adept at reading them. Not intellectually sophisticated enough to be distracted by what people say they mean, children learn how to act by observing what actually happens. They passively absorb an encyclopedia of human psychology before they learn to read. By the time they are old enough to realize that not all families interact the same way theirs does, they have pretty much been shaped by the values, attitudes, and behaviors common in their own. And because children are so closely bonded to their parents and so dependent on their parents' love and acceptance, their parents' relationship with them and with each other teaches them what to expect from love. What parents say and do, the behaviors they tolerate in themselves and in their children, establish the parameters of what is considered normal, acceptable, and desirable in someone who loves them. Besides, traditionally in our culture, children are taught to accept disrespectful treatment. Even good parents with the best intentions say things or act in ways that their children interpret as rejection. So when children are reprimanded for some transgression or criticized "for their own good," they are threatened by the withdrawal of their parents' love.

In the world of physics, we know that every action prompts an equal and opposite reaction. The same is true in personal relationships. We often assume that because children are powerless, they are incapable of reacting. But that's not the case at all. In fact, children usually end up modeling themselves after or rebelling against their parents. However, as children, it was difficult to fight back, so we learned to survive psychologically using a range of coping mechanisms. Maybe we silently pouted, whined incessantly, or screamed at the top of our lungs. Maybe we acted out our anger impulsively or held it in for days or weeks. Maybe we just learned to tune our parents out. Maybe we learned to lie. Or maybe we became consummate "good children," doing everything we knew would win our parents over to our side again. We eventually hit on some strategy that worked, that got us what we wanted or at least curtailed our parents' hurtful behavior toward us.

Families with dysfunctional dynamics not only teach but also reinforce the bad lessons. Our interactions with family members are essentially test sites for future relationships. When Daddy told Mommy that he loved her but then he ridiculed her, we learned that loving someone gives us the right to compromise her or his dignity. We may even have been invited or encouraged to join in the fun. When Mommy complained bitterly to you about Daddy's drinking but met him at the door each evening, martini in hand, we learned that it's normal, perhaps even best, to compromise our own convictions to keep the peace and make someone else happy. When Mom phoned Dad's boss with a story about his having the flu to cover for his hangover, we learned that lying is OK and that we—not he—should suffer the consequences of his actions.

Growing up, we encountered other people—relatives, friends, lovers, mates—whose family dynamics were probably no healthier than the dynamics at play in our own family. Through adolescence and the first tentative steps into the sea of love, we picked up a whole new set of unrealistic expectations and esteem-diminishing messages. Now suddenly, instead of vying for and dealing with one or two people whose love we already have, we find ourselves seeking approval, acceptance, and love in a world of strangers. It's not surprising, then, that we naturally gravitate toward people whose behaviors and attitudes seem familiar to us and feel comfortable—just like home, in fact. You may look at your middle-aged, mildly alcoholic father and your overachieving college sweetheart and see a world of difference between them. If you scratch the surface, however, and peer at what drives each of them, you will discover more similarities than you expected. Both may be too preoccupied to give you the love and attention you crave and are therefore emotionally unavailable to you. Even when we seek out potential mates whose behaviors and attitudes seem completely opposite those of our parents, more often than not we will find someone who treats us essentially the same way one or both of our parents treated us.

## Identify Your Mistakes

When we try to fix relationship problems by following the old instructions we picked up from family, friends, past relationships, and our own insecurities and fears, we seldom realize we are using the wrong tools. Without ever questioning our actions, we repeat the mistakes we've observed and then defend them whenever someone challenges us. For example, after someone treats you badly, you may try harder to make the relationship work. When your friends advise you to dump him, you defend him—and yourself—with excuses: "He's going through a bad time right now, and he really needs me." Before too long, he has hurt you again.

When our actions (our mistakes) don't work, we seem surprised and become discouraged. We even believe that nothing can possibly work—and I admit that in a few cases that may well be true. But for most of the clients I've treated, their problems have had solutions. And their first step in finding the solution was identifying the mistakes they were making.

You may be surprised by the true mistake behind some of these behaviors, but most of them should be obvious. You may find yourself wondering, *What's wrong with these women? Aren't they smart enough to figure it out*? If being smart were all it took, therapists would be out of business and everyone would live happily ever after. But as you may suspect by now, there's a lot more to it than that. Logic and intelligence do

| If You Find Yourself . . . | Because You Believe . . . , | You May Be Making This Dumb Mistake . . . | | | | | | |
|---|---|---|---|---|---|---|---|---|
| | | 1. Forcing Intimacy | 2. Expecting Him to Read Your Mind | 3. Playing the Martyr | 4. Assuming You Are Right | 5. Rescuing Your Mate | 6. Taking Your Mate for Granted | 7. Letting Passion Die |
| adopting his friends and interests while neglecting or giving up your own | you two will soon be inseparable and real love demands such sacrifice | ✓ | | ✓ | | ✓ | | |
| thinking, *He's not the person I thought he was* | he is a bad person | | | ✓ | ✓ | | ✓ | ✓ |
| trying harder than he does to make the relationship work | that giving him more will make him love you more | ✓ | ✓ | ✓ | | | | |
| flirting with and pursuing other men | he's not attracted to you anymore | | | | | ✓ | ✓ | ✓ |
| telling him what to do, how to do it, and when to do it | he won't do it right unless you direct him | | ✓ | | ✓ | ✓ | | |
| blowing up in anger and regretting it later | it's bad to express anger but then find you can no longer hold it in | | ✓ | | ✓ | ✓ | | |
| considering or actually having an affair | he will never be there for you and so you deserve to have your needs met elsewhere | | | | | | ✓ | ✓ |

| If You Find Yourself . . . | Because You Believe . . . . | 1. Forcing Intimacy | 2. Expecting Him to Read Your Mind | 3. Playing the Martyr | 4. Assuming You Are Right | 5. Rescuing Your Mate | 6. Taking Your Mate for Granted | 7. Letting Passion Die |
| --- | --- | --- | --- | --- | --- | --- | --- | --- |
| trying to get even with him | that he deserves to be punished and punishment will make him change his behavior | | ✓ | ✓ | ✓ | ✓ | | |
| calling, sending cards, and pursuing sex with little or no reciprocation | pursuing him will finally make him want you | ✓ | | ✓ | | | | |
| talking about him behind his back | he can't handle your feelings and you need to confide in someone | | ✓ | ✓ | | ✓ | | |
| staying busy to avoid the relationship | it's better to keep your distance than to fight | | ✓ | | | | ✓ | ✓ |
| whining or crying about problems in the relationship | life should be fair and easy | | ✓ | ✓ | ✓ | ✓ | | |
| openly criticizing, judging, and/or nagging him | that pointing out his problems will help him become a better person | | | | ✓ | | ✓ | |
| in battles over which of you is right and which of you is wrong | there is only one right way to do everything—and your way is the right way | | ✓ | | ✓ | ✓ | ✓ | |

| If You Find Yourself . . . | Because You Believe . . . , | 1. Forcing Intimacy | 2. Expecting Him to Read Your Mind | 3. Playing the Martyr | 4. Assuming You Are Right | 5. Rescuing Your Mate | 6. Taking Your Mate for Granted | 7. Letting Passion Die |
|---|---|---|---|---|---|---|---|---|
| | You May Be Making This Dumb Mistake . . . | | | | | | | |
| giving to the relationship more than you get out of it | the more you give him, the more he will love you | ✓ | | ✓ | | ✓ | | |
| blaming him for your unhappiness | you'd be happy if only he'd change | ✓ | ✓ | ✓ | ✓ | | | |
| constantly trying to help your mate in some way | he needs your help and it will make him love you more | ✓ | | ✓ | ✓ | ✓ | ✓ | |
| treating your mate like just a roommate | that sex and romance naturally diminish over time | | | | | | ✓ | ✓ |
| afraid to stand up to him | he's better and smarter and always wins | ✓ | ✓ | ✓ | ✓ | ✓ | ✓ | |
| attracted to down-and-out mates | you are stronger than they are, and they need your help | ✓ | | ✓ | | ✓ | | |
| continually getting upset that he's not meeting your needs | that if he loved you, he'd know what you need—you shouldn't have to tell him | | ✓ | | | ✓ | | |
| treating your mate disrespectfully | he's weak | | | | ✓ | ✓ | ✓ | |

not override our emotional reactions. The problems that plague and destroy relationships are not like the challenges you faced in school or at work. For one thing, someone consciously prepared you for these challenges. You were taught the best, most effective ways of identifying and addressing the problems you would encounter in those environments. When it comes to handling your relationship with your mate, however, you are actively, consciously taught nothing. The little you pick up is, at best, just plain wrong and, at worst, self-destructive.

## The Road to the Seven Dumbest Mistakes

There are many reasons why we make mistakes in relationships. One is that we embrace false beliefs that really don't work for us. Another is that our need for love, approval, and acceptance clouds our judgment. Myriad other reasons thrive in the untended bed of our unresolved issues: need to protect our egos, fear of conflict, use of old defenses, desire for challenge, and need to win. We usually force intimacy because we need love and approval as a result of having felt unloved in the past. When we expect our mates to read our minds, we are often acting out of a bad habit and out of false beliefs about love. When we play the martyr, we are often modeling behavior we saw in our mother and in other women. When we assume that we are right, we are protecting our egos, a behavior we may have picked up from our fathers. When we rescue our mate, we are often chasing after love and approval, or we may be implementing a response we learned by taking care of a needy parent or sibling. When we take our mate for granted, it is because we have learned that when someone loves us, he'll hang in there even when he's getting nothing from the relationship. When we break the sexual bond, we are often seeking love and approval outside our primary relationship, and we are probably behaving this way because we (along with our mate) have poor communication skills.

Most of us act out in these ways at one time or another, but we must recognize and reject the beliefs that accompany these behaviors because they are usually the culprits underlying our mistakes. Obviously, we cannot change the past. But we can learn how to identify the real cause of recurring relationship problems, the reason why we end up with the same type of mate again and again and make the same mistakes—we can learn to crack the code that masks the reason why we behave as we do, and we can learn how to break the cycle.

## Relationships Are Different Today

No question about it, relationships today are different from those of the past. Compared with our mothers and perhaps even with our older sisters, we expect more from our relationships, our mates, and ourselves. At the same time, our relationships demand more of us. Take Tricia, for instance. She juggles a career, a husband, and two young daughters. She expects her husband to be supportive and loving when she comes home. Both she and her husband have moved far beyond the traditional roles, and their lives would not have been functional, let alone fulfilling, if they had not.

Many of us find personal fulfillment in meeting the challenges of our different roles. If we're honest, however, we admit that keeping the mate, the kids, the clients, the boss, and the extended family happy involves quite a balancing act. In an ideal world, we would have all the time we needed to be a great mother, a respected professional, and a loving mate. But this is not an ideal world. There never seems to be enough time, whether we need an extra few hours for a long overdue romantic rendezvous or a few extra years to reset the biological clock. From hour to hour—even from minute to minute—

we shift emotional gears, going from office boss, to kitchen peacemaker, to bedroom siren, and back again.

Our expectations are different, too. Unlike women of previous generations, we do not cast our self-worth simply in terms of how successfully we marry and how many children we have. We are more likely to desire a healthy relationship for what it can do for us, for the ways it can enhance our lives and facilitate other goals in life.

## Men and Women Are Different, Too

Though most women do not think men are changing fast enough, both sexes are continuously evolving in terms of how they view themselves and what they want from life. For example, many young fathers today bond with their children actively, and some older men are starting a second family, thereby getting a second chance at being emotionally close. Men are also beginning to put more importance on the value and quality of their relationships. Daily life is a challenge for everyone, and these enlightened men are likely to seek balanced relationships with mates who will make them feel loved, cared for, and supported. Unlike the "quiet revolution" men have undergone, the changes we women have experienced have been phenomenal, highly visible transformations in terms of freedom, opportunity, and status. Over the past thirty years, women as a whole have become more financially secure, less willing to restrict our lives exclusively to the home, and less likely to tolerate bad relationships. At the same time, we, too, seek loving, supportive relationships in which we share equally.

Such relationships do not sound like much to ask for, and yet even when both partners want the same kind of healthy, balanced relationship, they often end up disappointed. They blame themselves or their mate when in fact the real culprits are the false beliefs and outdated attitudes they hold. Looking back, you can probably see how your tastes, opinions, and understanding have grown and changed. Yet most of us subconsciously think of men and relationships in the same terms we used to think of them when we were very young. Our attempts to build a new, balanced, and supportive love out of the old parts we pick up from old-fashioned, unequal, and nonsupportive relationships—others' and our own—are doomed.

Even now, with the sexual revolution and the rallying cries of feminism decades behind us, our ideas of what men and women are, should be, and should do remain in flux. However, the truth is that a healthy person of either sex combines qualities traditionally ascribed to both sexes: feminine understanding, empathy, and sensitivity and masculine confidence, ability, and strength. To make the new love work, women need to be soft yet strong: We do not have to abandon the old messages; we just have to elaborate on them. It is not only OK but also desirable to still say, "I don't want to hurt you, or believe that you want to hurt me." But for the sake of ourselves and our relationships, we must also show strength by saying and believing, "But if you do hurt me, I will not tolerate or accept it."

While we strive for equality, we also recognize important differences between men and women. There's no question about it: We *are* different in many important ways. Consequently, men and women rarely understand each other. Women think men are too logical; men find women too emotional. Women will say of someone who has taken advantage of them, "I would never treat anyone like that. Why did he treat me that way?" And they will often be even nicer to him in the hopes he will change. Men in a similar situation are more likely to end the relationship or refuse to be taken advantage of. They rarely see any benefit to learning why someone behaved as she did and cannot believe that a woman will continue being nice to someone who mistreats her. This is a complex subject, and there are exceptions to every rule, but generally speaking, men are solution oriented, whereas women are process oriented. Women tend to define success in terms of how healthy their relationships are. Men, on the other hand, view success as a measure of how much control they have over others. Women are raised to cooperate, to put others' needs before their own. Men are brought up to compete, to place their self-interest first. None of this makes men or women bad or better—it just makes them different. When we fail to recognize and accept the difference, we build up unrealistic expectations and guarantee we will be disappointed. And whose fault is that?

We also need to look objectively at some of our false beliefs about the sexes. Are men stronger? They commit suicide three times as often as women; they are twenty-five times as likely to commit and be imprisoned for crimes; their rate of drug addiction is significantly higher; they are many times as likely to assault or kill their partners and children. *Are* women the weaker sex? Hardly. The truth is that these false beliefs hurt all of us. The same stereotypes that dictated that all women are—or at least pretend to be—weak, docile, and submissive also cast men in roles that did not really fit them.

Until just recently, men have been forced to pretend that their emotions did not matter. When men do express themselves, open up, and reveal vulnerability, we sometimes react as if they have done something wrong, let us down, shown us that they're wimps. Few of us admit that when men do let down their guard, they threaten our sense of security. We say that they are too afraid to drop the mask, to show us the little boy behind the façade. But the truth is more complex: Many men have learned from experience that women are not really comfortable with a man who shares all his problems, his emotions, his insecurities, and his fears. He may also fear getting close to a woman because he can't bear

| The Top Ten Things Men Wish Women Knew . . . but Will Never Tell Them | The Top Ten Things Women Wish Men Knew . . . but Will Never Tell Them |
| --- | --- |
| 1. The more available you are to me, the less I want you. | 1. I want you to shower me with gifts, but if you do it too quickly, I'll think you're a geek. |
| 2. I often act macho because for my whole life I've been told that this is what you really want. | 2. I choose men who I think are stronger or better than I am; then I resent them for acting that way. |
| 3. I really do like strong women, as long as they don't use that strength just to bust my balls. | 3. When I'm able to get power or control in a relationship, I am as likely to abuse it as men are. |
| 4. I don't often talk to you because I think you really don't want to hear about my pain. | 4. I want you to be warm and emotional, but it scares me when you tell me your problems. I still don't believe I'm as strong as you are, so I need to know I can depend on you to protect me. |
| 5. I fear deep, intense relationships because I'm afraid I'll let you manipulate me, and that threatens my masculinity. | 5. Sometimes I know that I'm playing games with you, but I won't admit it. |
| 6. I feel powerful when I take care of you, but I lose respect for a woman who cannot or will not take care of herself. | 6. I want you to take care of me, but I don't want you to exercise the control that gives you over me. |
| 7. When I let you have your way, I sometimes hold it against you later. | 7. I wish you would stand up to me instead of appeasing me. |
| 8. Even though I say you're too emotional, your emotions make me feel alive when I'm with you. | 8. I want you to be emotionally open, but when you are not, I make excuses for you, think it's normal, and then complain about it. |

| The Top Ten Things Men Wish Women Knew . . . but Will Never Tell Them | The Top Ten Things Women Wish Men Knew . . . but Will Never Tell Them |
| --- | --- |
| 9. When I'm quick to say I'm in love with you, I'll probably be equally quick to leave you. | 9. When you are quick to say you love me, I'm more likely to start taking you for granted. |
| 10. Even though I act tough, I need love just as much as you do, and deep down I'm just as confused about how to find it. | 10. Even though I act tough, I need love just as much as you do, and deep down I'm just as confused about how to find it. |

being overwhelmed by his emotions, both good and bad. Men need the same things we do, but they fear the possible consequences of the openness and vulnerability they must exhibit to achieve them.

If we women are completely honest with ourselves, we know that we are sometimes unfair, that we say we want one thing when we really want something else. Although we say we are justified in behaving as we do and can build wonderfully logical arguments to support our case, deep inside we know when we are playing the spoiled brat or the princess. The pout, the scowl, the silent treatment, the dramatic gesture—we often know very well what will work and what won't. And although we may feel we've gotten our way, these are hollow victories that ultimately weaken and even kill our relationships.

## The False Beliefs That Undermine Real Love

Even when we know intellectually that we want relationships different than those of our parents, we often fail to apply that knowledge to our everyday lives because those beliefs are well engrained in us. For most of us, home was a showcase of stereotypical attitudes and behaviors: Dad did the important (that is, the money-earning) work while Mom stayed home and took care of us; Dad handled the finances while Mom shopped within the budget; Dad laid down the law while Mom threatened, "Wait till your father gets home." I'm not saying that every home was like this. Indeed, your mother may have worked outside the home or might otherwise have broken the housewife mold. Odds are, however, that when it came to the emotional and psychological responsibilities, your mother—not your father—was the caretaker, the problem solver, the advice giver—in a word, the nurturer. It was probably Mom who taught you, perhaps without ever saying a word, that the good of the greater entity—Dad's happiness, the family, her marriage—comes before her personal needs and desires, that self-sacrifice is necessary, even noble, and that to believe otherwise is not nice. These beliefs are often the bedrock on which unhealthy relationships are built. Clinging to them can cause us to reinforce a bad relationship that would otherwise crumble under its own weight.

Which of the following do you believe?

- You should expect to give more than you get out of life.
- It's necessary and admirable to sacrifice for those you love.
- If something feels good, it can't be all wrong.
- You should not say things that will hurt others.
- Anger serves no purpose and is best left unexpressed.
- The past is the past; there's nothing you can do about how it affects you today.
- Punishing your mate for bad behavior will make him change.
- In a relationship, each person's primary obligation is to make his or her mate happy.
- True love is magical and doesn't take much work.
- Justice will prevail; what goes around comes around.

- There is a clear difference between right and wrong, and most people know what it is.
- People who are in love with each other agree on most things.
- There are good people and bad people in the world.
- Love conquers all.

You are probably familiar with most of these beliefs and may even ascribe to one, some, even all of them. These concepts are extremely powerful and pervasive because they are drummed into us from an early age by parents, teachers, religious leaders, and society at large. They feel right because they're familiar. They appeal to us because they simplify complex issues, reducing everything to black and white.

And that's precisely why these are not good guidelines: They teach us how to live in a perfect world, one that does not exist. Out of desperation, we sometimes find ourselves pining for the so-called good old days, when these teachings, it is said, reflected a better, kinder, simpler world. Don't believe it! Life never was—and never will be—simple. Nostalgia for the past embraces only the ideal of times gone by, not the reality. The beliefs listed above reflect the fantasy of how we wish things could be, not how they ever are.

This is not to say that all these ideas are wrong all the time. They are not. Sometimes it is noble to sacrifice for those you love. Sometimes justice does prevail. And very rarely, punishment yields the desired result. The problem arises when we integrate these ideas into our worldview and use them—rather than common sense, emotional awareness, and psychological understanding—to dictate our decisions. When we do this, we substitute a fantasy world for reality. Casting our problems and their possible solutions in these absolute terms only dooms us to fail. When we blindly defer to these beliefs, we put ourselves at a grave disadvantage. It's like trying to play Monopoly with Scrabble tiles. We can never win.

## The New Rules for the New Love

It is wrong to think that we can fashion a new, healthy relationship on the false, traditional beliefs. We see the problems

---

### The Sixteen Essential Elements of a Healthy Relationship

1. allowing yourself to be vulnerable, to admit your own weaknesses, and to recognize and openly admit when you are wrong
2. allowing yourself to get in touch with and express a full range of emotions, including anger
3. feeling and expressing love, admiration, and respect for your mate
4. having high self-esteem
5. communicating regularly, from the depths of your soul
6. continually bonding through experiences, such as reminiscing about the past, planning for the future, playing and having fun together
7. having intensely emotional sex
8. demonstrating the willingness to address issues and negotiate solutions
9. setting and respecting each other's personal boundaries
10. taking responsibility for your own life while being supportive of your mate
11. being willing to try new things in life, both with and without your mate
12. recognizing your first signs of resentment and speaking up so that you can constructively address the issue together
13. living so that each of you is an asset to the other's life, instead of a liability
14. making and keeping a long-term commitment to each other
15. assuming the best rather than the worst about your mate without being naïve
16. continually reminding each other of your love

our parents had or those we ourselves experienced in prior relationships, but we tend to lay the blame for them on one or both partners' behavior. In fact, most of the problems we encounter in relationships derive from the beliefs these relationships are based on. We all make mistakes; none of us is perfect. Unhealthy, traditionally structured relationships exacerbate those mistakes and allow little room for improvement or change. If anything, these relationships actually thrive on unhealthy dynamics. In contrast, the new relationship nurtures and supports expression, equality, fairness, and consideration.

To have the relationship between equals that we deserve, we need a new set of beliefs and teachings, ones that reflect the issues we face today and encourage us to have the relationships we want now. One piece of good news is that a new, healthier, more realistic way of viewing women, men, and their relationships is evolving. The other piece of good news is that our generation is at the forefront of this seismic change. *Where's the bad news?* you might wonder. I don't believe there is any, but I will tell you that to have the relationship you want and to keep your love alive, you must make a serious commitment and a great effort. And it is all within your power if you are willing to work at it. Before we chart our new course, let's look back at how we got to where we are.

**2**

# Relationships 101:
# Why We Do the Things We Do

## We Make Mistakes Because We Carry Baggage

Time and again I hear women complain of their mates' baggage—their experiences from the past that shape how they think and feel today. The expression "too much baggage" is a cliché describing a very real and common problem. We are all products of our past, and we've all had bad experiences with former lovers, parents, siblings, friends, and co-workers. When we don't bother to face these issues, process them emotionally, and put them behind us, they cannot help but affect our current relationships.

## Our Past Relationships Were Out of Balance

### *Old Defenses Cause Us to Make Mistakes*

As children, we were all hurt at times. Because we lacked the power to defend ourselves—to speak up, to influence the people and situations that hurt us, to escape, if necessary—we learned other ways to protect ourselves. We may have withdrawn or cried or covertly plotted revenge. These behaviors are normal in children, even necessary to their development. By the time we enter late adolescence, however, we should have expanded our emotional repertoire beyond whining, pouting, withdrawing, and manipulating others. We should be learning a new set of skills, including standing up for ourselves, addressing our problems, and confronting the people who cause them. Unfortunately, most of us do not learn to set personal boundaries because no one bothered telling us that we should and we so rarely see others doing it. We simply internalized more of the false beliefs. For example, we expect others to treat us fairly of their own accord, out of the goodness of their heart, because they know it's the right thing to do. When they don't, we play the martyr. We get upset and find ourselves facing the only two options we ever learned to consider: Stay and take it, or leave. No one ever told us that we can renegotiate the terms of a relationship or that there are healthy ways to persuade others to treat us well.

Sometimes you may get it half-right: You try to stand up for yourself or assume you are right and overcontrol your mate to avoid being overcontrolled yourself. Other times, incidents from your past may cause you to experience emotional flashbacks whenever someone says or does something that makes you feel the same hurt you felt as a child. Flashbacks can cause you to try to force intimacy to get the love you wanted from your parents. Or you may try to rescue your mate, since, for example, you were unable to rescue your alcoholic father.

Subconsciously, we all seek balance. At the same time and without even realizing it, however, we set up relationships that are perennially out of balance and unhealthy. We might think of ourselves as bookkeepers and our relationships as separate accounts. Ideally, each should balance at the end, with our investment and the other person's coming up pretty much equal. But in real life, that rarely happens, and what we end up doing—even though we seldom realize it—is using a new relationship to correct the imbalance of a previous one. We are like the bookkeeper who finds that an old account is ten dollars short and decides to make it up by taking the money from a new one. It never really works since, for one thing, that old account is closed. In the end, extracting some payback from the current mate to compensate for an earlier wrong only depletes the new relationship.

Another way we try to balance our new books is by withholding the trust, the love—the emotional capital—we should be investing. We think that if we save it in this way, we won't put it at risk, and to some extent we are correct. But again, all we have done is shortchange our mate and ourselves. In love as in business, an undercapitalized venture is doomed to fail.

## The Balancing Act

Good, sound relationships allow and encourage partners to strike and maintain a balance between them. This is not to say that every conflict ends in a win-win resolution or that each party always meets the other exactly halfway. What it does mean is that when we focus on the relationship as a whole, we find that while each partner is firm about personal boundaries and identity, between them is an ebb and flow of compromise, consideration, and effort.

### We Try to Balance Opposites

Every relationship involves two people, each of whom plays a different role. Both contribute to the relationship's dynamics with what they do and say, with how they feel and make the other person feel, and through the values they bring to bear. Because we base so much of our behavior in relationships on values we learned as children, our relationships inevitably conform to a pattern based on one person's having more control than the other. There are different ways of describing this relationship: victim-controller or parent-child, for example. I prefer to use the terms *controller* and *dependent*. Here *controller* is shorthand for the person who usually makes the decisions, assumes responsibility, and defines the relationship, and *dependent* describes the person who yields all his or her power in these areas to the mate. Although there may be differences in degree, virtually every relationship conforms to this pattern. The inherent imbalance of the controller-dependent relationship lies at the heart of each of the Seven Dumbest Mistakes.

Generally, we do not consciously choose the role we assume; it just seems to happen. I say "seems to" because there is always an element of will involved. If there were not, these patterns would be impossible to break, and they are not. Camille grew up watching her father hurt her mother and thought, *Poor Mom—Dad's a jerk,* and began to empathize and identify with her mother. In doing so, she subconsciously chose the dependent role. On the other hand, her sister Michelle witnessed the same interactions between their parents and concluded, *Mom's so weak and Dad's so strong. He doesn't seem to feel as bad as she does.* She then subconsciously adopted the controller's role. Somewhere between the two extremes of controller and dependent (Dad and Michelle, Mom and Camille) lies a healthy middle ground. As you can see from the chart on page 28, for example, it is healthy to desire intimacy, but the problem is in how we respond to and act on our need for it. If our desire for intimacy makes us *fear* it, we are likely to be controlling; if our desire makes us *crave* intimacy, we are likely to be dependent. The extreme behaviors are equally unhealthy, whereas the middle ground—seeking closeness but setting boundaries (for ourselves and others) that don't allow suffocation—is healthy. According to the characteristics listed, which role do you most often assume?

## Are You an Emotionally Controlling, Dependent, or Healthy Person?

| Controlling | Dependent | Healthy |
|---|---|---|
| fakes strength | believes others are stronger | knows we all have strengths and weaknesses |
| expresses anger, but avoids the expression of vulnerable and tender feelings | is too vulnerable and avoids the expression of angry feelings | expresses both vulnerability and anger |
| hides true self from others | exposes too much of self to others | opens up only as much as partner does |
| fears intimacy, therefore avoids it | craves intimacy | desires and seeks intimacy within boundaries |
| adopts authoritarian attitude; tries to control others | complies with outside authority; gives up control to others | maintains authority and control over own life, not over others' lives |
| denies personal problems | feels burdened with "too many" personal problems | recognizes and solves personal problems |
| is emotionally constricted | is emotionally overreactive | expresses the emotional response appropriate to each situation |
| blames others for problems | blames own inadequacies for problems | holds self and others accountable for their actions and words |

Controllers and dependents come in pairs, for good reason: Opposites *do* attract. You cannot play either role without the presence and participation of your opposite, your foil. People often ask whether it's "better" to be dependent or controlling. Neither role is healthy. Both roles cause you to make mistakes in your relationships. Both roles prevent you from fully seeing yourself and how you contribute to the problem. Since you cannot begin to change what you do not see, playing either role limits your ability to change while fueling guilt and/or resentment, emotions that often poison love.

Dependents are likely to make mistakes that involve giving up control, such as playing the martyr and expecting their mate to read their mind. Controllers usually make mistakes that involve wresting control from others, such as assuming they are right, rescuing their mate, and taking their mate for granted. Both dependents and controllers can be guilty of forcing intimacy and letting passion die. You will see which role you play most often as we examine the Seven Dumbest Mistakes in greater detail. Understanding dependent-controller dynamics is key to avoiding future mistakes. Although we generally assume that all controllers are men and all dependents are women, the truth is that not only can each sex play both roles, but in many relationships, partners switch back and forth between roles. Or in an attempt not to be dependent, as she was in her last relationship, a woman may begin a new relationship as a controller. In a classic example, a woman whose father abused her mother will be more likely to choose one of the two equally unhealthy alternatives demonstrated at home. Like Camille and her mother, she may become the dependent of a controlling mate, or like Michelle and her father she may become the controller of a dependent mate. We are emotionally healthy and more likely to attract healthy mates when we settle into the midpoint between these two extremes.

Identifying the controller and the dependent in a relationship is not always simple. Take Scott and Ann, both in their early forties and typical of the couples I see in therapy. They argue about many things, but each complaint ultimately boils down to its all being the other person's fault. When I begin therapy with a couple, I speak to each person separately so that

I can understand how he or she sees the situation. My job is then to help each one recognize the mistakes each is making. Here is the kind of argument Scott and Ann often have:

SCOTT: "You said you wanted to be a landscape designer, so I paid for the schooling. But now, once again, you've decided that you don't want to work in that field. I try to help you, but I can't win."

ANN: "I wasn't that good at it. You even criticized my work. Besides, why should I work? You make enough money."

SCOTT: "Money is not the point. Besides, I only criticized your work so that it would improve. Why are you so insecure?"

ANN: "You sure don't help matters! You constantly try to control me, and you're doing it now. I've changed my mind about wanting to do landscaping, so stop bugging me!"

SCOTT: "I don't care what you do. I just want you to do something that you're good at that makes you happy."

ANN: "I *am* happy. Who said I wasn't happy? All I need to be happy is a husband who talks to me and cares about me."

SCOTT: "I do care about you, but I don't have the time to constantly worry about your feelings and whether or not I'm talking to you enough. That's why I want you to get some outside interests that make you happy. I don't care if it's a job or a hobby—just do something."

ANN: "I do plenty—or didn't you notice who does your laundry and cooks your dinner? Doing things on my own isn't going to make me happy. I want a husband who wants to do things *with* me—who likes me and respects me."

SCOTT: "I do like you, but I don't respect how you spend your time. Housework isn't important; I can always pay to have that done. I want you to do something you enjoy. I can't keep taking your pressure to be in a good mood and talk to you every night after putting in ten-hour days at the office. I need you to get off my case!"

ANN: "Fine! I will!"

And with that, the two generally went to bed angry.

Can you see who is controlling and who is dependent here? Most women will clearly see that Scott just doesn't get it, that he's controlling Ann and telling her what to do. Most men, on the other hand, will probably identify with Scott. They will see Scott's frustration in this no-win situation. After all, he is just trying to help Ann, not control her. Women probably feel sorry for Ann and understand her neediness and her frustration, but few probably see how she is playing an equal part in destroying her relationship with Scott. Sometimes we have trouble recognizing and identifying problematic behavior because we are blinded by certain gender-based assumptions.

Let's look more closely at how both Scott and Ann are harming the relationship and making several of the Seven Dumbest Mistakes. Ann is contributing to their problems through her dependent behavior. Scott is right when he accuses Ann of pressuring him (*forcing intimacy*). He's also right when he accuses Ann of not making herself happy. Ann has adopted a needy posture and has informed Scott that the only possible remedy depends on his doing what she believes he should do, thereby indirectly blaming him for her unhappiness and *playing the martyr*. Her constant finger-pointing and whining make him not want to spend time with her.

When Scott avoids her, he thinks she should know why; he's *expecting her to read his mind*. Ann is also right about Scott not spending quality time with her (*taking her for granted*) and trying to control her (*assuming he's always right*). But Scott's biggest mistake is trying to solve her problems for her (*rescuing his mate*), and then resenting her when it doesn't work. He acts like a parent and treats Ann like a child when he speaks to her in a condescending, disrespectful manner. He says he doesn't respect what she does with her time, but that's only part of it. The fact that he talks about her even as he is talking to her indicates general disrespect. Although Scott believes he's doing something positive by trying to take care of Ann, he is actually putting her down. After all, it is the belief that she is weaker than he is that ultimately motivates him to take care of her. If he truly believes she is a responsible adult and his equal, he would tell her how her behavior is affecting him—without protecting her—and then assume she is strong enough to handle the problem herself without his constant direction.

Both Scott and Ann feel unappreciated by each other. It seems that Ann doesn't appreciate the value of a dollar and how hard Scott works to earn money, and Scott obviously doesn't value Ann's contributions in the home. They are both *taking the other for granted*.

For this relationship to get back on track, both Scott and Ann must change. You can see how Scott's *rescuing* and Ann's *martyrdom* fuel each other in a vicious cycle, creating a dysfunctional balance. But the cycle can be stopped. Here's how: When Ann decides to *stop playing the martyr* and stand on her own, take responsibility for her own happiness, and set boundaries about what behaviors of Scott's (like his criticizing her, telling her what she should do, and avoiding her) she will and will not accept, he will see her as stronger and will have less incentive to rescue her. And if he is not rescuing her, he will be less likely to view her as someone who is incapable, someone who is not his equal. Once he is no longer trying to make Ann happy, he will have less opportunity to exert control. Once Ann no longer feels controlled by Scott and feels his respect for her, her childish behavior will have outlived its usefulness. Also, when she is making herself happy, she won't need to *force intimacy*. Scott is staying away because he can't stand her neediness. Once her neediness is replaced with emotional independence, Ann will be happier and more attractive to Scott, and with him no longer in the position of having to take care of her, he will admire her and want to be closer to her.

## Reasons We Make Dumb Mistakes

### *Unresolved Hurt Makes Us Fear Closeness*

The singles' world is filled with men and women who feel so deeply wounded by past relationships that they will not risk ever getting close to anyone else. If you ask these people whether they fear closeness, they will deny it. After all, they might point out, they put a lot of energy into finding new relationships. Once in these relationships, however, they hit a wall they can't seem to break through to connect with the other person. Even married people often unknowingly distance themselves from their mate. Their intimacy comfort zone doesn't allow their mate to get very close because of their unresolved issues. Yet just because they are married or their involvement is passionate, volatile, or compelling, they think that they have an intimate relationship. Often they are surprised to find out that their mate has emotionally bonded with someone outside their relationship.

When we fear closeness, we put ourselves in a double bind: We crave intimacy desperately, yet subconsciously we sabotage it. We've all had bad experiences, ranging from being the victim of physical or sexual abuse to being the target of critical comments. Though consciously we want to believe otherwise, deep inside we see the moral of the story as this: Getting close to others causes more pain than it's worth. To undo this lesson, we must reexamine our experiences and figure out how we could handle the same situation differently today.

## *Replaying Old Tapes Causes Repeating of Choices*

"Why do I keep finding men who want me only for my money?" You are probably making the mistake of rescuing your mate or playing the martyr.

"Why do all the men I meet want to take over my life and tell me what to do?" You're playing the martyr and probably expecting your mate to read your mind.

"Why is it that every time I fall in love, it's with a guy who just won't take responsibility and make a commitment?" You're probably trying to force intimacy.

Sound familiar? Doesn't it amaze you when you realize this new guy is so much like the last one—especially since you swore you would never date anyone like that again? We often repeat a pattern of picking mates who eventually prove to be just like those who came before. I say *eventually* because many times we are attracted to people we feel comfortable with but seem just different enough to make us think, *He's so different.* As we learn too late, the differences between this new mate and past ones are matters of style, not substance. He may be more sophisticated or more considerate or more attentive than your last mate but ultimately equally immature, controlling, abusive, or whatever other characteristics typify your pattern.

Time and again I've heard women berate themselves, moaning, "Why don't I ever learn? I really do want someone who's different. I don't want to go through this again." Yet chances are the next relationship will be very much like the last one, and so on, until the pattern is broken. The first step in avoiding the same type of mate is to realize that you keep choosing that type.

The second step is to try to understand why you make these choices. Underlying your behavior is a history of unresolved issues. Women who successfully resolve the issues of past relationships do not feel compelled to deal with them again in future relationships. Those who do not resolve those issues, however, lock themselves into a pattern, replaying the story in the hopes of getting a happy ending this time. Consciously, a woman may sense that the potential new mate spells trouble. Subconsciously, however, she regards him as another chance to rewrite the script. Ironically, the more bad endings her relationships have produced, the more she will invest in seeking the same type again, hoping to find that one relationship that will break the pattern and vindicate both her and her beliefs (among them that justice does prevail, that love always saves the day, and so on). Unfortunately, repeating relationships doesn't break patterns. People do.

### Unfinished Business Causes Us to Chase Approval and Rejection

Do you put more energy into your relationship than your mate does? Do you often think he's better than you are? Do you worry about making him happy? Are you attracted to potential mates who make it clear that they don't want you? Do you then find people who are attracted to you boring or uninteresting?

If you answered yes to any of these questions, you are probably chasing after approval. Our natural needs to be loved and accepted drive us to form relationships and bonds. In itself, this drive is healthy. Without it, we would have no meaningful social interaction, and life would not be worth living. Seeking acceptance takes on the unhealthy form of chasing after approval when it leads us to behave in ways that undermine our self-interest, our self-esteem, and our relationships.

When we continue to chase approval after someone repeatedly rejects us, we are also chasing after rejection. It sounds rough, and it is. Chasing someone's rejection is the most common reason we make mistakes in relationships, and it's serious. It also often contributes to or keeps us from correcting our mistakes.

## We Won't Let Go of People Who Are Bad for Us

Joanne's fiancé, Evan, grew increasingly distressed over her ongoing relationship with her ex-husband, Darryl. After two years of marriage, Joanne had left Darryl because of his philandering. Now, five years later and just months before Joanne and Evan's wedding day, Darryl was calling to elicit her commiseration about his latest breakup. After talking to Darryl for an hour, Joanne then recounted the conversation to Evan, stressing how bad she felt for Darryl and wondering aloud what else she could do to help him. Evan finally complained the next time Darryl called—at three o'clock in the morning—and Joanne got defensive. Their argument:

JOANNE: "You just don't understand, Evan. Darryl has no one else. No one understands him the way I do."

EVAN: "Yes, but your marriage ended five years ago. And he's not exactly what I would call a friend. The only time you ever hear from him is when he has a problem."

JOANNE: "I know, but look how well things turned out for me; I have you. Poor Darryl doesn't have anyone. Just because we're divorced doesn't mean I have to cut him out of my life. I would think you could be more understanding."

EVAN: "Me? Are you kidding? This is the ninth or tenth time this has happened, and I've been pretty understanding so far. But I have to tell you, Joanne, I don't want this to go on after we get married. I really feel that if you really loved me and were really ready to commit to our marriage, you could make the break with Darryl."

JOANNE: "Oh, stop being so jealous! This is ridiculous!"

When Joanne and Evan came to me for counseling, she offered me the same excuses she gave Evan: Darryl really "needed" her. Evan was right to confront Joanne about an issue that was making him feel uneasy. And, as I pointed out to Joanne, she was not only continuing to stay involved with Darryl because he needed her. The truth was that she needed to keep helping Darryl to assuage her own guilt for leaving him. It's no wonder that her current mate wondered whether she wasn't still in love with Darryl. After all, Darryl kept drawing her attention, and Joanne kept making room for him in her current relationship.

When we feel pity for an ex or feel guilty about how we behaved in a past relationship, or when we keep chasing after someone's approval after the relationship ends, we are attempting to right some wrong. Unfortunately, this often comes at the expense of a current relationship. One example of this syndrome is the woman who continues to play the martyr by regularly inviting her abusive ex-husband to her home even after she's told her new boyfriend that she still fears her ex. Or, like Joanne, who regularly talks on the phone to her ex-mate—because she feels sorry for him (and is still trying to rescue him)—even when her current boyfriend is visiting.

We tell ourselves that we are just being nice. Perhaps. But the truth is that guilt, anger, or other emotions from our past are keeping us locked in to a pattern of being manipulated by people from our past. These past relationships need to be resolved. Besides, when these relationships are not resolved, they crop up whenever a similar issue arises in our life again.

## We Don't Recognize the Real Consequences of Our Beliefs

In the previous chapter, I discussed the false beliefs that often cause us to make mistakes. It is generally easy to understand why these beliefs don't work in healthy relationships. What is harder to see are their real consequences. We often cling to them because we have learned to expect a certain result. For example, Kate wanted to believe that justice always prevails. She kept acting on that belief by being good and making sacrifices for others, particularly her underemployed boyfriend,

Ray. After six years, Kate came into my office very depressed because Ray was leaving her. As Kate learned the hard way, justice does not always prevail, and we end up squandering our time, energy, and emotions on flimsy, unrealistic goals.

We can avoid these problems by myth busting—learning to recognize and then redefining our false beliefs in terms of their real-world consequences. Instead of telling yourself the fairy tale—for example, "The more I give him, the more he will love me"—stop and remind yourself of the real outcome of your actions: "The more I give him, the less he will respect me."

| The Myth | The Bust |
| --- | --- |
| Love demands that I give up my interests and friends and adopt his. | If you lose your identity, he will lose interest. |
| I shouldn't have to tell him what I want; if he loved me, he would know. | He will probably disappoint you if you don't tell him how you feel, and what you want. |
| The more I give him, the more he will love me. | The more you give without reciprocation, the more he will take and ultimately lose respect for you. |
| I hold my anger in so I won't hurt him. | Holding anger in instead of expressing it as it occurs causes you to explode or build resentments, which ultimately destroys the relationship. |
| I talk about him to others because he can't handle my feelings, and I need to tell someone. | Telling others allows you to convict him without giving him the chance to understand your feelings and change his behavior. |

| The Myth | The Bust |
|---|---|
| If only he would change, I'd be happy. | Only you can make yourself happy; if you change your behavior, he will have to change. |
| He always wins because he's better and smarter than I am, so what's the point of standing up to him? | Because he is intimidating, you let him win by backing down. |
| Life should be fair and easy. | Life is not fair; you must create your own justice by going after what you want. |
| Pointing out his problems to him will help him become a better person. | Criticism damages his self-esteem and makes him resent you. |
| There's a right way and a wrong way to do everything. | There is no one right way, and when you refuse to recognize that, you are showing disrespect for your mate and his beliefs. |
| Punishment makes people change. | Punishment builds resentment. |
| He needs my help because he can't do it on his own, and ultimately he'll appreciate it. | Your constant "help" tells your mate you don't believe he can cut it on his own, a judgment he can't help but resent. |
| Sex and romance eventually wane, no matter how much you love someone. | Sex and romance do not die naturally; they are killed by neglect. |
| Some people are just bad. | People exhibit bad behavior, and bad behavior can be changed. |
| It's better to keep your distance than to fight. | Distance creates walls and problems. Unresolved, it poisons your relationship. |

# How to Stop Making Dumb Relationship Mistakes

## *Identify and Admit Your Mistakes, and Vow to Stop*

Most people are in such denial about their own behavior that they lack the awareness to make changes. When we assert that our problems are not all our fault, we are correct to a certain degree. We go wrong when we begin thinking that not being completely at fault relieves us of the responsibility to do anything to correct the problem. Any time you relinquish your responsibility, you throw away your power to control, influence, and change your life. You are the sole constant in every relationship you will ever have. Everyone and everything around you may be wrong, but until you change, nothing else will.

## *Separate Your Identity from Your Mate's*

It feels good temporarily to be enmeshed in our mate's life, just as it felt good when we were young children and believed our parents could do no wrong. It's hard to separate ourselves from others psychologically. When we do not complete the separation from our parents and/or our former mates, we continue needing their love and approval. This emotional dependency pushes us to seek mates and relationships that replicate the parent-child, dependent-controller model rather than a healthy, balanced man-woman partnership of equals. Rather than develop a romantic relationship based on equality and mutual respect, in the dependent-controller relationship we trade in our identity and our share of control for his love.

As long as we participate in relationships in which we are playing the role of controller or dependent, we will instinctively make the same Seven Dumbest Mistakes. To stop making these mistakes, we must psychologically separate ourselves from people who play the opposing role, including lovers, friends, or our parents. This separation requires that we pull away and get angry enough to stop playing our role. Unless we complete this task, we will be chasing after our opponent's approval—or someone else's—indefinitely.

To claim your own identity, you must become self-reliant and learn to go against the grain, defy unreasonable authority, and worry less about what others will think of you. Instead of always blindly accepting that others—be it parents, a religious group, an expert, anyone—know better than you do what is right for you, you must learn to question them, ignore their approval or disapproval, and begin to trust yourself.

### Admit Your Mistakes to Your Mate, and Require Him to Do the Same

When you admit your mistakes to your mate, you are making yourself vulnerable to him; you are letting him know that you care and that you want the relationship to work. Once you admit your mistakes, you are also letting your mate know that he may monitor your bad behavior and ensuring that you won't be forgetting the part you play. To maintain balance, be sure he does the same for you.

### Know Yourself

When you know who you are and how you really feel, you'll be less likely to repeat your mistakes. Spend time alone staying in touch with your feelings, needs, wants. Look into your childhood and your past relationships to figure out your patterns, the issues and behaviors that really upset you (push your buttons), and the reasons why you are the way you are. Then vow to be your true self around others instead of who you think they want you to be.

### Express Your Feelings and Wants

Most of us were taught that it's selfish to tell people how we feel and what we want. As a result, we usually express ourselves indirectly and hope that our mate can figure out what we really mean. We must learn to express our feelings and wants directly, using the Four Steps to Healthy Communication (see page 80).

Developing an intimate relationship requires emotional honesty. Emotional honesty involves expression of your full range of emotions—from tears to anger. Without this, your mate can't really know you.

## Establish and Respect Your Own Boundaries

There are probably things your mate and others in your life are doing that hurt you. You may respond by nagging those people, avoiding them, or getting defensive in a variety of ways. These behaviors are counterproductive for two reasons: They never solve the real problem, and they often exacerbate your resentment and anger over the real issue. Instead, you need to learn how to set boundaries and communicate them clearly to those around you. In setting boundaries, you artic- ulate what behaviors are unacceptable to you and what con- sequences will ensue if those boundaries are crossed. A boundary may concern your mate's being fifteen minutes late for dinner, or it may concern him slapping you. What it con- cerns is not as important as the fact that you state your posi- tion and, if and when the boundary is violated, you carry through with the consequences no matter how seemingly minor they may be. People who set boundaries and are known to stick to them are less likely to be abused or to have reason to feel resentment.

## Resolve Issues from the Past

You cannot change the past, but you can change whether and how it affects your current relationships. Cleaning up baggage from the past gives you the strength and the confidence that put and keep you in charge of your own life. It also helps you better guard against reacting to the baggage of old lovers, parents, siblings, or friends. Resolving past issues may require writing letters to former lovers, setting up meetings with family members, or reviewing a bad situation with the help of a therapist. In an ongoing relationship, it often involves going over the resentments you and your mate have built up over time and finding better resolutions for the future, a topic discussed in Chapter 8, "Taking Your Mate for Granted."

## Be Willing to Take Risks

Without risk taking, you cannot change your behavior or your life. But let's be honest: It is difficult to change because it's more comfortable to repeat the past than to venture into the unknown. Saying that we repeat the past is really something of a misnomer. What we usually repeat is the role we were assigned or the role we played in our family and in previous relationships. For example, my client Cynthia grew up in a home where everyone yelled. To her, yelling and being yelled at are normal. That is not to say she likes it, but it is what she knew, and she brought this behavior to her relationships, with disastrous results. Another client, Paula, was raised in a family where people were considered bad or selfish if they expressed anger. Now whenever a man becomes upset over anything, she automatically thinks there's something wrong with him. At the same time, she whines to anyone who will listen that others mistreat her, yet she never says or does anything to stop this behavior. Both these women failed to realize that what they were raised with, what is familiar to them, is very powerful. To change, they— and you—must be willing to try new behaviors and new ways of looking at things, even if these innovations do not at first feel normal or right.

## *Control Yourself, Not Your Mate*

We always want to change *him*. We think that we would be happy if only *he* did this or *he* did that. The truth is that by changing your own behavior, you will affect his. Instead of expecting George to read her mind, Tina told him she wanted orchids on her birthday. Instead of trying to force Nathan to care about her and feeling frustrated and rejected because he never pursued her, Rita took my advice. She backed off so he could pursue her. When your behavior is healthy, others have only two options: Respond in a healthy manner, or stay away from you.

## *Build Intimacy*

Set aside time for the relationship, time to talk, touch, share, laugh, and even fight. The sharing of both good and bad feelings builds intimacy. Sharing successes as well as handling crises together builds a bond that no one else can destroy. Do not let work, children, family, friends, or unresolved issues tear your relationship apart. Develop an attitude that says, "It's you and me against the world."

## A Last Word on Relationships

No matter what brings a new client to my office, the first question I always ask is "If I could wave a magic wand and make your life exactly the way you want it to be, what would you want?" The answer is almost always some variation on "a happy relationship (along with more money)." Unfortunately, I do not have that magic wand, but I do have the tools to give you that you can use to realize your dream. In this book, I will give you those tools and a clear understanding of how to use them. I know from clients who have learned to avoid the

Seven Dumbest Mistakes that the results are so wonderful they seem almost magical, and in a way they are. This new kind of magic, however, is based in reality, not on fairy tales. Its power derives from truth, not from secrets or illusions. And it requires your full and complete attention and participation. It is within your power to change yourself and turn your relationship into what you want it to be—creating your own magic.

## PART TWO

---

# THE SEVEN DUMBEST
# RELATIONSHIP MISTAKES:
# HOW TO STOP MAKING THEM

# 3

# Mistake Number One: Forcing Intimacy

Years ago I went through a phase where I was afraid to get close to men. Ironically, the more emotional distance I put between myself and the men I knew, the greater my hunger for instant intimacy. When I did meet a man I liked, one of us—usually me—rushed the other into intimacy. The pattern usually involved forgoing other people and personal interests to spend time together, having sex very early on, and one or both of us idealizing the other to the point where we convinced ourselves we'd found "the one." Of course, neither of us was really in love—to be honest, we barely knew each other—but we thought we were because the relationship was intense and exciting, and I admit, I loved it. When the relationship burned itself out—as it always would—I never understood why because I did not see the mistake I was making.

At the same time I realized these "quick" relationships never had time to build, so I knew there had to be a better way. I maintained a detailed fantasy of my perfect relationship.

First, the man and I would meet in the hallway at work and just say hello. Then we might chat at the water cooler, and a few days or weeks later one of us would suggest, "Let's have lunch someday." Over the next few months, we would talk in passing, have lunch, eventually becoming friends and talking about love, life, work, relationships, philosophy, sports, hobbies, politics—whatever. Then we would plan our first date, a Saturday-afternoon hike or an early-evening dinner out, preferably on a day when one of us had to be someplace else afterward. We would move toward greater intimacy slowly, with a first kiss, a lingering hug, and then a special night. And so would begin a long-term monogamous relationship, one we could look back on and honestly say was neither rushed nor forced and about which we each made our own decisions without pressure from the other.

I called this scenario a fantasy, but by then I'd learned enough about psychology and relationships to know that for couples in strong, happy relationships, this is no dream. This is really how their love begins. Still, knowing this did not stop me from continuing to chase that wildly exciting infatuation stage of intimacy that I thought was love.

## Why Emotional Intimacy Is So Important

Emotional intimacy is the heart of a good, healthy, long-term relationship; it is the one element without which real love cannot survive. True intimacy develops over time, and although the timing varies from couple to couple, true love *never* happens overnight. When we say "intimacy," most of us automatically think "sex." But there is much more to it than that. True intimacy involves the expression of both positive and negative feelings, the revelation and consideration of our own and our partner's strengths and weaknesses. True intimacy provides a shelter in which we can be vulnerable and open, feel safe, and truly be ourselves. Within the confines of a truly intimate relationship, the real lifeblood of love—honest, open communication—flows.

Forced intimacy distracts us from the work of building a real bond because it lulls us into thinking we have already achieved it. It's interesting to note that the telltale signs of forcing intimacy—chasing after approval and pursuing potential lovers, fantasizing about them in our future, having sex too soon, and giving up our identity—strike many people as normal, even romantic. The all-consuming whirlwind romance, the pursuit and capture of the one we can't live without, the irresistible hot chemistry that lands us in bed on that first date—that's the stuff of best-selling books, hit movies, and long-running soaps. But in real life, it's the stuff of shattered dreams, loneliness, and depression. Why? Because forcing intimacy *never* produces the healthy relationship people want.

Think about happy couples you know and how they met. There is a very good explanation for why so many couples meet at school or at work and why, though wrong, people often fall in love with their best friend's spouse. The best love develops gradually, as you get to know someone. That is not to say you may not meet someone who has his own reasons for responding to forced intimacy. It is possible to build a relationship on forced intimacy, but it is rare and seldom becomes a healthy, supportive relationship.

## Why Forcing Intimacy Is a Mistake

As true intimacy develops, both partners move closer at about the same pace, neither one feeling pressured or pushed. Forced intimacy, in contrast, feels unnatural and uncomfortable to the partner being pursued. Instinctively at some point, he will withdraw, which only sends you the signal that you need to try harder to win his love. Forcing intimacy is unhealthy and self-defeating because it makes you dependent on his approval. As long as you seek and pursue his love, he will be in control. In addition, when you force intimacy, you threaten your intended mate's personal boundaries, and it is natural for him to feel frightened and to respond by withdrawing from the relationship or rejecting you. Whether you're in pursuit of a relationship or in one in which your emotional needs are not being met, trying to force intimacy is always a mistake. Not only will it not produce the intimacy you want, but it will also push your mate (or your potential mate) further and further away.

## Why We Force Intimacy

### We Have Not Resolved Past Rejection

Kim, a twenty-nine-year-old physical therapist, never had a relationship that did not begin with her forcing intimacy. When she became my client, she was separated from her second husband, Tony, and she was desperate to figure out where she kept going wrong. In her case, the root of her intimacy-forcing behavior was easy to uncover. She was an only child and her father's "little princess." Because her mother was often distracted with her acting career, Kim and her father were very close. When she was fourteen, however, her parents divorced, and two years later Kim's father remarried and began a new family.

Kim, formerly a model student, became boy crazy. She dated dozens of boys and never understood why they dropped her as soon as they had sex with her. Only Roger, who married her right after they graduated from high school, seemed to care. But after two years, he tired of her needing to be with him every minute, and they divorced. When Kim met Tony, she was sure everything would be different, but after a year he, too, was ready to walk out. In one session, Tony complained that he was tired of being responsible for Kim's happiness and sick of hearing about what a great guy her father was. Several times that day, Tony felt compelled to remind Kim that she hadn't seen her father in over a year and that he'd been too busy to attend their wedding. In Kim's eyes, however, her father could do no wrong.

When you make the mistake of forcing intimacy, it is almost always because, like Kim, you have a need for love and approval from your childhood that has not been resolved. Women who force intimacy are often chasing after the approval of their emotionally unavailable fathers through the men they date, although it also could be that they're seeking the approval of their mother, siblings, or ex-mates. It is difficult to stop making this mistake until you have gone back and resolved the issue with whoever you felt rejected by emotionally.

## We Fear Being Alone

We are brought up to believe that everyone should be part of a couple, so if we are alone, we assume there must be something wrong with us. We are so taken with the idea of couplehood as a perfect state that when we find ourselves between relationships, we assume there is a reason why we were not chosen for happiness. Are we unlovable? Undeserving? Bad? Given our image of aloneness, it is not surprising that some of us will do anything to avoid it.

## We Crave Intimacy Yet Fear It, Too

People who are the most terrified of intimacy and commitment are usually the ones most likely to force intimacy. This does not seem logical, but if you look at the reasons behind the behavior, it makes perfect sense. Because people who frequently force intimacy seldom experience long-term relationships, they are constantly hungry for intimacy. This is why they, especially men, are likely to engage in premature sex and why they want to spend vast amounts of time with a woman at first. Once they have gotten their fill of intense intimacy, however, they turn around and decide that they're being suffocated, and they bolt. After a while, they meet someone new and start the same pattern over again—forcing, then fearing intimacy.

Rushed relationships are built on pretense, not on true intimacy. At the beginning of any relationship, most of us are on our best behavior and careful to present our best side. Sooner or later, though, reality sets in. If you have established a pattern of forcing intimacy, it may be because you actually fear true intimacy. It's almost as if you tell yourself, *The sooner I reach my goal—relationship, commitment, marriage, baby, you name it—the less time he'll have to really know me.* It is interesting that people who fear intimacy often unknowingly attract others who fear it, too, and the cycle continues.

## We Want the Fairy Tale

The drive to love and to be loved, to be deeply, emotionally connected to someone else, is our fantasy, and that fantasy can be overpowering. In itself, it is not a bad thing; the problem lies in what we do to fulfill it. When we rush to find a quick fix instead of doing the work necessary to build a deep, stable relationship, it's like eating cake instead of steak. It's more exciting but ultimately leaves us unsatisfied. Rushing into a relationship, having sex too soon, giving up our identity to our partner—all these are ways of keeping the fantasy alive and spinning. In allowing so much to happen so quickly, we guarantee we will not have time to think about the person we are involved with, what he's really like, how the future with him would really be, how we really feel. When this whirling merry-go-round finally slows—as it eventually will—and we take our first good look at the fairgrounds, suddenly everything seems different—not as colorful, as bright, or as real as we believed it was. The fact is, though, nothing and no one changed. We just finally began to see things as they really and always were.

That first call, the first date, the first dance, the first kiss, that first night—the words alone evoke an aura of mystery, excitement, and pleasure. Each new first is a step into the unknown, an emotionally intense experience, an adrenaline rush that lingers long after almost everything else about him is forgotten. When these events occur in rapid succession, they are even more exciting, and this is another aspect of forcing intimacy, one that some simply cannot resist. But what goes up must come down, and so will you.

This is especially true when you have sex too soon. In the instant intimacy of sex, you feel loved, appreciated, valued, and wanted. No wonder you make the mistake of believing this is really love when you should be telling yourself, *This is just sex*. Sex is intense physical intimacy, and with someone you barely know, that is all it is and all it can ever be. If you remind yourself that your partner's intensity probably has more to do with his own need to be loved than with any love he may profess for you, it will be easier to avoid making more of the experience than it is. This is not to say that he may not be attracted to you or that he may not enjoy being with you at that moment. He might feel these things, and so might you. But these feelings apply only to that moment, and they tell you nothing about your long-term prospects.

## How We Force Intimacy and How We Can Stop

Learn to recognize how you force intimacy or allow others to force it on you; then commit yourself to changing this destructive, no-win pattern. The key is learning to recognize and avoid these telltale patterns.

## We Chase After Approval

Whenever you put considerably more time and effort into a relationship than your mate does, you send the message that you are not worthy of or equal to him, that his lack of involvement and his lack of reciprocation are acceptable, and that you will tolerate his neglect and possibly even his abuse indefinitely. Chasing after approval often comes attractively dressed up in false romantic beliefs. In the beginning, you may convince yourself that this is it, the big, once-in-a-lifetime romance you've been waiting for, and so it's OK, even admirable and romantic, to drop your guard. As the relationship progresses, you may tell yourself and others that all you are doing is trying to make him happy, protect his ego, and nobly sacrifice your interests for him. Deep inside, though, you know that you're investing more than he is. And you probably resent it. You should.

How do we get to this point? From early childhood, we naturally seek approval. When our parents and, later, other important people in our lives didn't give us that approval, we interpreted that to mean we were not OK, we were inadequate and unworthy, and so we wanted to prove them wrong. Now, because of this, when someone new rejects us or pulls back from us, we instinctively feel compelled to change his mind, to prove him wrong, to show him that we are good enough to warrant his esteem. When the person rejecting us is someone we love or regard as a potential mate, that drive becomes even stronger, often undeniable. We often speak of how others push our buttons, but usually this "rejection button" is the key one from our past that sets off sometimes uncontrollable anger and pain, which can be alleviated, we think, only by the hard-won acceptance of the person who is now rejecting us.

Though it seems to defy logic, the more someone indicates that we have not won his approval, the more we will invest in proving him wrong. Whether we like it or not, this creates a bond between us and the person who is ignoring, rejecting, or otherwise telling us that we don't count. Instead of simply rejecting *him*, we are drawn to him by an attraction too often mistaken for love. And so we embark on an ever-escalating spiral, trying to win approval that will never come. Ironically, in his eyes, the harder we try, the less worthy we are. The relationship eventually crumbles anyway, but as long as it lasts, our craving his approval ensures that it will never be a partnership of equals. In chasing after his approval, we relinquish control, become dependent, and push him further away.

## How to Stop Chasing After Approval: Reverse His Rejection

When you chase after someone's approval, you become dependent and give him the controller role. You also create a self-defeating scenario more conducive to his rejecting you than to his ever approving of you. To reclaim your power in the relationship, you need to reverse the rejection. In other words, examine your past intimacy-forcing behavior, and resolve to take the opposite course in the hope of getting him to chase you.

It's difficult to change your behavior when you instinctively feel that forcing intimacy is right. Admit that you are seeking the attention, love, and commitment of someone who either is not as interested in this relationship as you are or wants only an unbalanced relationship in which he can call the shots. If you do try to reverse his rejection and the relationship ends instead, you can walk away certain that the problem was his, not yours.

Women sometimes find difficult the idea of rejecting someone they care about. We worry that if we start doing a little rejecting, too, we may lose him, be less good, or become as bad as the person rejecting us. Some of my clients

| If You Force Intimacy By . . . , | You Can Reverse His Rejection By . . . |
|---|---|
| phoning him repeatedly, even though he does not return your calls | not calling him again until he calls you, and then waiting a few days before returning his call |
| giving him gifts he fails to acknowledge or reciprocate | sending no more cards, letters, or gifts and not acknowledging his |
| feeling compelled to see and talk to him every day | getting busy with other things and other people and ignoring him |
| talking about him to people he knows | appearing somewhat disinterested in what his friends say about him |
| accusing him of ignoring you when he's not constantly available | being sure you have less time for him than he has for you |
| feeling that whenever you're together, you're the last thing on his mind | resolving to spend only quality time with him and leaving his presence when he is not focused on you |
| making excuses for his bad behavior toward you | holding him accountable, clearly telling him why you don't want to be with him |

insist that reversing the rejection is playing games, something they prefer not to do. My feeling is that you can call it whatever you like; the bottom line is it works. If you feel uncomfortable about reversing rejection, admit it. But remember, you will never change his intimacy-avoiding behavior unless you first get his attention and he then becomes invested in you. To do that, you've got to make him do some chasing.

## *Don't Idealize Him; Don't Be Intimidated by Him*

No one is perfect. We know this of ourselves, and we generally believe it of others. Yet we sometimes fall for a man because of the image he projects, then blame him later for not being what he seemed.

> Fran had been seriously dating Gerald for about a year when their relationship ended suddenly. She came to my office confused and at a loss to determine just went awry. They had met at a mutual friend's wedding, on a yacht, and at first sight, Gerald seemed everything twenty-five-year-old Fran had dreamed of: handsome, successful, and mature. At forty-five, Gerald was, he said, in the process of divorcing his wife. To Fran, who had dropped out of college to try her hand at acting, Gerald was worldly and sophisticated, the perfect catch. When Gerald asked her to move in with him after a few months, she jumped. Her acting career was going nowhere, and she was tired of working as a part-time legal secretary.
>
> At first, living with Gerald was exciting. They attended gallery openings, hung out with his writer and artist friends, and spent their weekends combing antique stores, listening to classic jazz albums from his vast collection, and watching foreign films. Gerald never mentioned his soon-to-be ex-wife or his kids, and she never asked. She told her friends what a relief it was not to have to listen to a man talk about his failed marriage or his feelings. He never pressured her to do anything with him but be on his arm whenever they went out, and she was more than happy to oblige. Every few weeks, Gerald would treat Fran to a three- or four-day weekend at a luxurious spa out of town, claiming he would be wrapped up in work and urging her to go without him. The previous month he had treated her and her sister to a week in Saint Thomas.
>
> Of course, sometimes Fran wondered exactly what Gerald's business entailed, why he seemed to work only a few hours a day, and why he seemed to know everyone, but

his phone never rang. The entire time she knew Gerald, they never once went out with another couple socially, nor did they entertain at home.

When Fran asked whether she could invite her sister and mother over to celebrate her birthday, he talked her out of it, saying he wanted to make it "our special day." Fran, certain this meant he was going to propose, made arrangements to see her family for lunch the day before.

The evening of her birthday, Fran was almost bursting from anticipation. Waiting for Gerald, she began daydreaming about their wedding, the children they would have . . . That evening he came home and asked her to move out. He was going back to his wife.

"I just can't believe it," Fran kept repeating. "He seemed so perfect, and he acted like he wanted to marry me." Or so Fran told herself. In fact, however, Fran did not really know very much about Gerald at all, and she had been happy to keep it that way. Rather than press Gerald for details about his relationship with his wife or the progress of their divorce, Fran assumed the divorce was proceeding. When he was not forthcoming about his business, his friends, or other aspects of his personal life, Fran chose to believe what she wanted to believe. She fully accepted Gerald as he presented himself. Whatever nagging doubts she had initially frightened her because they threatened to tarnish his perfect man image.

Over time, Fran eventually saw that she thought Gerald was going to propose because that's what she had chosen to believe, just as she had decided to believe that Gerald was getting a divorce. Fran had fallen for the Gerald he wanted her to know—and the man she wanted him to be. Fran later realized that she had never really known Gerald at all, in large part because she didn't want to rock the fantasy world she had built up around him.

Most of us present our best face when we first meet someone. As the song says, we accentuate the positive—and we downplay the negative; there is nothing dishonest about that. When we fully believe someone else's first-date façade, we're likely to let him assume control. When we convince ourselves that someone else is perfect or closer to perfect than we are, we are more likely to want his approval. And chasing after approval causes us to make the mistake of forcing intimacy.

Like Dorothy discovering that the man behind the curtain is not really a wizard, we feel betrayed. *How could he be such a jerk?* we wonder. *How could he be so dishonest?* If we look carefully, however, we will see that by buying into someone else's image, we set ourselves up not to notice or discover anything that would conflict with what we want to believe.

You can protect yourself from this trap by subtly changing the way you think about a potential mate. As you review these points, keep in mind that the goal is not to build a case against your mate but to take him off his pedestal and maintain a balanced, realistic picture of who he really is.

- Just as you keep a mental list of what you like about him, also keep one of what you don't like.
- Realize that the more effort someone puts into convincing you that he is better than you, the less he probably believes it himself.
- Remind yourself of your strengths and his weaknesses.
- Find out about, and don't forget, his insecurities, fears, and personal problems.

### We Are Obsessed with Future Hopes and Dreams

When you meet a potential partner, do you immediately size him up as marriage material? Is the ticking of your biological clock too loud to ignore? Do you look at your present life— your job, your friends, your home—and think how great life will be when everything changes (that is, when you marry, have kids, and so on)?

It's natural and healthy to have goals and dreams for the future, and most of us would include a fulfilling, long-term relationship among them. These expectations become a problem, however, when we try to force a mate or a potential mate to fit into our fantasy by making him more than he really is. The belief that we can change a man after we marry him is one variation on this theme. Another is deliberately overlooking the signs that he might not be or even want to be our dream man, as Fran did.

When we focus on future expectations, we often damage whatever real relationship we might have had. I remember years ago, whenever I met a man I liked, I would phone all my girlfriends and exclaim, "This is the one! He's handsome, intelligent, rich, and I can picture us together forever!" I would idealize my new love so completely that I ignored anything about him that didn't fit. Needless to say, problems did not disappear simply because I ignored them; they got worse until the relationship ended. Focusing on your future expectations of a relationship is destructive in two ways. First, it can keep you in an unhealthy relationship. Second, it can blind you to ways that you might improve a relationship that is worth saving.

## Learn to Be Happy with Yourself Today—and Tomorrow

Remember, you will not be any happier in a relationship than you are alone. Try to look at a potential mate as an addition to—not a replacement for—your own life. A relationship can complement and add to your happiness, but it cannot create a sense of self-worth or well-being where there was none before.

Accept the possibility that you may not find the right relationship, that you may live forever as a single person. Face the fear; then move beyond it. Plan for a future alone, and picture yourself happy and fulfilled without one permanent mate. If you are now married, to experience the idea of making your own happiness, take some time alone and imagine yourself being OK as a single person.

## We Have Sex Too Soon

It would be impossible to count how many times I've heard women sitting in my office lament, "I know I slept with him too soon, but it felt so right. Now I can't believe he hasn't called me back." Men often make this mistake, too, though the two sexes usually respond to the experience in opposite ways. She usually feels that she is falling in love and wants only to be closer to him. He, on the other hand, is often frightened by the emotional intensity of the experience and feels compelled to get away from her.

Women seem to have a hard time understanding why the better the sex is, the greater the odds are that he won't call back. It does not seem to make sense, and it is not fair, but hearing it from thousands of men has convinced me it's true: Men do think less of a woman who appears to have been around or is too easy. Yes, they are frightened by the intensity, the instant intimacy of it all. But there's more to it. Just as women dream of the man who will father their children, so men also carry an image of their future wife and—most important here—the mother of their children. Countless cultural and psychological forces come into play here, and you can call it whatever you like—the old double standard, the Madonna (and I don't mean the singer)–whore complex; it boils down to the same thing: Most men don't value anything that comes too easy, and they are appalled by the image of their children's mother as sexually experienced and eager.

Even in the best of circumstances, however, having sex too soon makes both partners vulnerable. A woman who has sex too soon sets herself up to chase after the man's approval and force intimacy. The man in this situation is likely to be pressured to continue a relationship (or commit himself to a deeper relationship) that he may not be prepared for. Either way, a healthy relationship rarely emerges from this scenario.

Over the past few decades, we have come a long way toward freeing ourselves from unhealthy attitudes about sex. That is a good thing, but there is a downside as well. With the advent of safe, effective birth control, we have also been told that "everyone is doing it" and that if we are not, something must be wrong. One result is that we often find ourselves having sex with people we do not know as well as we probably should. However else we may think of sex—fun, spiritual, transcendent—we must accept that expressing and sharing ourselves sexually requires the ultimate degree of vulnerability. And while we may say that it's "just sex," deep inside we feel that having sex requires more and should mean more than sharing a meal or just going out on the town.

One client of mine, twenty-three-year-old Yvonne, had repeated a pattern of having sex with men after only a few dates even though she confided that she felt "weird" about it. Yvonne had reservations about her behavior, and when I asked her why she had sex despite them, she replied, "Well, guys just expect sex. Besides, if I like a guy, I don't want him to think I'm not interested. If he does, he'll go find someone else." I told Yvonne that when most men pressure women for sex early in the relationship, what they really want to know is whether or not they are attractive to the woman they're pursuing. I suggested to Yvonne that the next time she finds herself being pressured to have sex, she say, "I'm very attracted to you, but at this point I'm not comfortable rushing into sexual intimacy."

Most of us believe that the emotional intimacy outside the bedroom should equal the sexual intimacy inside it. When we have sex too soon, the imbalance between the two intimacy levels creates awkwardness and pressure that a new relationship simply cannot withstand. If we are honest, we know that neither we nor the new man really knows exactly how one feels about the other, yet the sexual intensity allows no room to step back and evaluate things objectively. Both partners either fake the emotional part—by pretending to like the other more than he or she does—or one simply pulls back until the level of emotional intimacy catches up to the level of sexual intimacy. Of course, the other partner often reads that as rejection.

This is not to say that having sex too soon never results in long-term relationships. Sometimes it does, but seldom are they healthy. One obvious example is the couple whose premature sexual relationship results in pregnancy and either a quick marriage or a lifelong, nonromantic relationship based on their mutual parenthood. When a couple feels like they "had to get married," it sets a negative tone for the relationship, and neither partner can look back and be sure there was not some ulterior motive all along. She may think, *Sex is all he wants, and I feel like an object,* while he may think, *She sure was sexy then but isn't now. Did she have sex with me just to trap me into marrying her?*

### How to Put Sex Where It Belongs: Invest in the Relationship Slowly and Gradually

Do not have sex with a man until and unless he is emotionally invested in you. Earlier I described my fantasy of how a great relationship would begin. After years of forcing intimacy, I finally got a chance to approach a man differently, and it really worked. It all began much as I imagined, only I didn't meet Alan at work but in a bar. We met, then he left. I didn't see him again until about three months later, when we ran into each other in another bar, and we talked. We liked each other immediately, but he was married, so neither of us pursued the relationship. Over time we kept bumping into each other. We would talk, and I got to know him a little through mutual friends.

It was not until eight months after we first met, when Alan told me he was leaving his wife, that we made plans to get together. I made clear that there would be no sexual intimacy until he had completely moved out of his wife's house and filed for divorce. I kept that boundary, although it was difficult at times. We saw each other only once a week for the next couple of months and didn't consummate our relationship until Alan had filed divorce papers and moved into his own apartment. For the first four or five months we dated, we each continued dating others. Finally, we brought up the subject of commitment and monogamy. The rest—some nine years later—is history.

We took our time falling in love, and the result is a deep bond no one can break. Our secrets? We didn't have sex too soon, and neither of us forced intimacy. During the first months we knew each other, we discussed various subjects and learned to respect each other as equals. Alan first learned to know me as an intelligent and valuable friend. I first learned to know him as a warm and considerate human being. And that's not to say there was no electricity between us—there was! But we held out, and now I can say it was worth the wait.

### We Give Up Our Identity to Live in Our Mate's Shadow

Carl came into therapy because his girlfriend, Rhonda, was pressuring him to move in with her. He told me he didn't think he loved her, but he didn't know why he felt that way. After all, Rhonda was the type of a woman he "should" want to be with, and since he was newly divorced, he welcomed all the attention she lavished on him.

So what was wrong? If we go back to the beginning of Carl and Rhonda's relationship, nine months before, we can see the patterns that were set from the start. Rhonda decided early on that Carl was the man for her. After just a few dates, she talked and thought of nothing but him. She ignored her girlfriends and family, her outside interests and responsibilities, to spend every weekend with Carl. And she made sure Carl would be available by scheduling dates and keeping the romance hot.

At first, it was easy for Carl to go along with Rhonda's plan, but now he was having second thoughts. She was shocked when he said he didn't think moving in together was a good idea because he wasn't sure he loved her.

"We were getting along so well together!" she replied. "If you didn't love me, why did you stay in the relationship?"

"Why not?" he answered. "It was fun."

In spite of starting out on the wrong foot, they saved their relationship, but it was not easy. When Carl admitted he was unsure of his love for Rhonda, he was not just being evasive. In pursuing him so intently, Rhonda had never given him either the opportunity or the need to meet her halfway. We rarely value what comes easily, and Carl realized he had never made a conscious decision to be with Rhonda.

Rhonda had to pull back from the relationship—stop calling, stop chasing, stop being available—and give Carl space to come toward her. She was reluctant to do this and understandably afraid he might discover he really didn't love her and end it. But she knew this was a chance she had to take. She let Carl know that she needed him to call her more often, plan more dates, and show her that he cared about her. He agreed to try. Once Rhonda stopped chasing Carl into a corner, he realized how much he did care for her. Given the chance to shoulder some responsibility for their relationship, he soon realized he did things for Rhonda because he wanted to, not because she demanded them. Once Carl demonstrated a willingness to participate fully in the relationship, Rhonda was less compelled to pressure him into making a commitment. With the pressure off both of them, love really bloomed.

It can happen so fast that you don't even realize you are giving up your identity. You meet him on Friday night, have dinner Saturday night, go boating with him on Sunday, meet his kids on Wednesday, then go with him to a party the next Friday. Each time he calls with new plans, you quickly scuttle whatever commitments you made before, leaving friends and family behind. Whenever a client tells me about her new, exciting life, I always warn that she risks losing her identity, to which she usually responds, "What identity? I didn't like my life before I met this guy, so what am I really losing?"

Each of us has a personality, an identity that is uniquely ours. It is important to remember that it was that identity—who you are, what you do, what you think—that attracted him to you in the first place. Appearing to have common interests, for example, can make a relationship click. But there's a big difference between being two separate people with interests in common and becoming two people with one identity—usually his.

Merging one's identity with one's mate's is something men and women both do, but more often than not it is the woman who drops her friends, her social life, and her interests to accommodate his. Typically, this does not seem like such a bad idea in the beginning, but no matter how much someone may say she is "choosing" to go along, eventually she will see her choice for what it really is: sacrifice of herself and abandonment of her own interests.

Despite protests to the contrary, a man really cannot force a woman to make these sacrifices. She makes them because she chooses to. For example, married couples and others in long-term relationships very often give up their identities to each other. In fact, this is what has occurred when you hear partners complain of being bored with their mates. A husband will tell me, "We don't socialize anymore because she never liked any of my friends," without realizing that he chose to give up those friends. A wife will say, "He didn't like it when I spent Saturdays skiing with my friends, so now I have nothing to do that I really enjoy." She, too, must recognize that she chose not to go with her friends. Either one of them could have stood up and tried to renegotiate the relationship—he might have found a way to see his friends less often or without her; she might have gone skiing every other weekend.

You might think that the woman who abandons her own identity to assume her mate's is the only unhappy partner. In fact, the partner whose interests seem to dominate the relationship also ends up feeling used and unappreciated. Years ago, I began dating a man who forced intimacy with me and eagerly gave up his identity. He did not have much of a social life, and I had a full calendar, so we quickly fell into a pattern whereby he accompanied me to engagements and get-togethers. He seemed to enjoy it and never declined an invitation or suggested alternatives. I felt I'd found someone who fit perfectly into my life until six months later, when he announced, "This relationship is over. I'm sick and tired of doing everything your way and letting you run my life!"

I was surprised and angry. Neither of us had ever told the other how we really felt. Frankly, I was tired of always making the decisions about what we should do and where we should go without getting any input from him. I felt he should be thankful to me for including him in my social life. And I resented his handing over the control, then blaming me for the sacrifices I never asked him to make on my behalf.

## Protect Your Personal Identity

You can best protect your identity in a relationship by doing the following:

- Refuse to alter aspects of your personality to please your mate. For example, do not tolerate others' bad behavior because your mate feels these transgressions are no big deal; do not stop voicing your opinions on controversial topics just because they make him uncomfortable.
- Continue to spend time with your friends and family.
- Include him when appropriate, but do not feel obligated to include him in everything you do.
- Continue to pursue your outside interests and hobbies. If you two share interests, great. But don't give up those you do not share (and don't ask him to do so).

- Do not reveal any personal dirt—such as the story of your abusive ex or your bout with alcoholism—until he has revealed some of the more private, less flattering aspects of his own life.

### We Allow Controllers to Force Intimacy

Even when we think we are not forcing intimacy, we may be making this mistake by allowing someone to force intimacy with us. Beware of those who give you the rush.

Marlene, an attractive thirty-five-year-old, came to see me after another romance fizzled. She had a history of forcing intimacy with men, but this time she had conscientiously avoided her usual pitfalls. She waited three months before she had sex with Richard, she refused the urge to call him constantly (as she had done with others), and in other ways kept her distance. Now she was confused because despite her efforts, this relationship had met the same unhappy end. Why?

She told me, "I met Richard through a dating club. I figured that men who join those must be serious about finding a long-term relationship. [By the way, Marlene's assumption is wrong.] I was afraid I had made a mistake with him when I slept with him before he said he loved me. It seemed like magic with us, and I was sure he was the one. He was attractive, my age, and had money and a house in an expensive neighborhood that I practically moved into.

"Gradually, however, he began to make little criticisms of me and my behavior. He tried to control me, like telling me he didn't think I should have another drink or asking me why I planned to do certain things certain ways. I listened to him and thought he was probably right. I began to put him on a pedestal. I felt so lucky that a strong, successful man like Richard had chosen me. I had been looking to buy a house, but I put that plan on hold and began to fantasize about living with him in his big, beautiful house.

"I tried to be everything he wanted me to be. I admired that he seemed very sure of himself and very clear about what he would and would not tolerate in his friends. He had no friends, but I thought that was just because he had these high standards. The fact that he had never had a serious long-term relationship with a woman I also attributed to his being so particular. And, to be honest, that made me feel [I was] even a little more extraspecial in his eyes.

"Then one night, about three months into the relationship, I saw him flirting with another woman at a cocktail party. When we got home, I confronted him about it. He told me I was just being possessive and jealous. Then he accused me of being so drunk that I saw it all wrong. I felt bad, apologized, and asked him to forgive me. He said he didn't know if he could forgive me and thought he needed a break from me. I begged him to work it out with me. He said he'd call me in three weeks.

"I beat myself up terribly during those weeks because I felt like I had really screwed up. When we finally did talk, he said that his feelings had changed and that now he just wanted us to be friends. He said he could never forgive me for the way I acted and added that he didn't really think we were right for each other anyway. I was devastated! I asked him, 'What about the good times we had?' He said he had fun, too, but I wasn't the right woman for him. I just couldn't understand what happened."

You can probably identify the ways in which both Marlene and Richard forced intimacy: fantasizing about the future and having sex too soon (even though Marlene waited longer than usual, he had not made any emotional commitment to her). In addition, Marlene idealized Richard and gave up much of her identity and her independence to be part of his life. Although Marlene had avoided some of the mistakes she had made in previous relationships and Richard was the one doing the chasing initially, the results were discouragingly similar. She was so swept up in his world that she didn't even realize she had given up her identity again. She let her fantasies about Richard blind her to the truth about him. For example, he was not "particular" about people; he was immature and critical, something Marlene realized only when he began criticizing and trying to control her. Yes, they had spent a great deal of time together, but when Marlene looked back, she saw that Richard never came to her house, met her friends, or shared with her emotionally. Her fear of being alone again had prompted her to make excuses for his behavior. Eventually, she saw that Richard was the needy one who had forced the intimacy that weakened whatever bond they felt initially.

### Stop Starving Yourself for Intimacy

People force intimacy because they are not getting their needs for intimacy met in other relationships and in other aspects of their lives. When we get discouraged, frustrated, or depressed, we withdraw. Soon we are not going out as often or keeping in touch with friends and family members, which only makes us feel more depressed. Then, not wanting to let on how bad we feel, we withdraw even further from those who do care about us and from those whom we really need the most. We end up lonelier, needier, and more susceptible to forcing—or being forced into—intimacy.

## Always Know When to Pull Back

There are times in every relationship—even the best ones—when you have to look closely at your behavior and pull back to rebalance things between the two of you. By *pulling back,* I mean refocusing your energy, directing it away from him. Don't just stop calling him and then pine away for him. Actually stop making him a priority in your life. Take that trip to Mexico with your girlfriend, treat your niece or nephew to a

day at the zoo, consider accepting the transfer you've been offered at work. When you pull back, assume that the relationship is over, and begin moving forward without him. If you
are married, let your husband know what you are doing and
be sure he understands that you are not happy with the relationship. Tell him what you want from him, give him a deadline, then pull back and leave him alone until then.

Remember that if you move toward someone and try to
force intimacy, you leave him no choice but to move away

---

### Eight Tips for Women Who Want an Intimate, Bonded Relationship

1. Don't have sex too soon. Make sure you take time to know each other.
2. Always tell him what you want from him and from the relationship *and* what you will do if you don't get it.
3. Don't give him the power to make you feel great about yourself. When you do, you give him the power to make you feel bad about yourself as well.
4. Make it a condition of your relationship that he be as open and honest with you as you are with him. At the first indication that he is not, stop revealing yourself.
5. Don't give more time, energy, love, or commitment than you get.
6. Don't make the relationship too easy for him. When you do, you are telling him that you value him more than you value yourself.
7. Start the relationship by encouraging the treatment you want and discouraging the behavior you do not want. Remember, actions speak louder than words. People infer what you want from what you accept. If you accept bad behavior, don't be surprised when it continues.
8. Be soft yet strong; feminine but competent. Don't hide your strengths or diminish your accomplishments. Be sure he falls in love with the real you.

from you. If you do this, it doesn't mean there's anything wrong with you; it simply means that you are making a Dumb Mistake. You can change your behavior, reverse the rejection, and get him chasing after your approval. And once you do that, it's very likely that you may look at him more realistically and decide he's really not the one for you. If he is the one, though, this time you will have begun building your relationship on a strong foundation.

# 4

# Mistake Number Two:
# Expecting Your Mate to Read Your Mind

Marcy, thirty-eight and never married, had just walked out on Gus, her boyfriend of the past eight months. In my office, she complained that she would never have a good relationship because "there just aren't any good men out there. I might as well give up.

"I feel that I'm a very strong, private person. No one knows my business. I never let any man make me cry, and I never really get angry," she said proudly. "I left Gus for several reasons. First, he has no manners. He eats like a pig. He's rude to my friends sometimes, and he didn't invite me to go with him on a weekend camping trip with him and his buddies. Of course, I never discussed any of these things with him. He should know how I feel. If I did tell him how I felt, I know it would hurt his feelings.

"I've been a little distant with him and sometimes withdrawn. But he didn't ask me what was wrong or anything. I've learned from my father and other men I've been involved with that men don't change, so why bother? Now that he's gone off on this camping trip without me, well, that's it. It's over!"

By the time Marcy came to me, she had built a strong case against Gus based on these issues and his "obvious" lack of concern about her feelings. The catch here was that the only person with the power to change Gus's behavior—Gus— had no idea how Marcy felt. Marcy had made one of the Seven Dumbest Mistakes: She expected her mate to read her mind, and he "failed."

## Charades: A Losing Game in Love

"He should know how much that upsets me."

"Why can't he try to figure it out? Why do I always have to tell him?"

"The guy can't take a hint."

"If he *really* loved me, he'd know what I mean."

Sound familiar? Every one of these comments insinuates that a mate should be able to understand what a woman is thinking and feeling without her having to utter a word. We are raised to think that we become stronger when we suffer in silence, swallow our anger, and allow people to live their own lives—even when these actions compromise our values and our self-esteem. In fact, however, choosing not to communicate in a direct, healthy manner is weak, cowardly, and sometimes even two-faced. No matter how you may rationalize why you do it—"I'm protecting his feelings," "It doesn't really matter," "He won't change anyway, so why bother?"— withholding communication *never* improves matters. Worse, it never gives your partner a chance to defend himself, to explain why he does what he does or to see your point of view and possibly change. Women often say that they want things to change, but how they expect that to happen when they rarely reveal what they want puzzles many men and, I admit, some therapists.

## Why Communication Is Important

More than sex, more than romance, more than friendship, more than anything else, communication is the heart of love. When we fall in love, no matter how close we get, we remain two separate individuals. Only communication bridges the gap between us. It is impossible to avoid occasional lapses in communication. Unfortunately, when we withhold communication, we deprive ourselves, our mate, and our relationship of the only effective means of solving whatever problems we face and building the intimacy we desire. When we choose not to communicate clearly and directly—and this *is* a choice—we are relinquishing our responsibility and control in the relationship.

## Why Expecting Your Mate to Read Your Mind Is a Mistake

There are many reasons why expecting your mate to read your mind is a bad strategy, but the first, most obvious one is that it is doomed to fail. When you expect your mate to read your mind, you are being unfair to him (because he will rarely stumble on the magic answer) and to yourself (because you ensure that you will never get what you want and will always be angry about it).

Communication is so essential that the moment a couple starts miscommunicating, a predictable chain of events is set in motion, like a row of toppling dominoes. When you do not express yourself fully, you are bound to be misunderstood. And when you feel that no one understands you, you hold in negative feelings and resentment. Eventually, these feelings calcify into a case against your partner that, although one-sided, is compelling simply because it leaves no room for his defense. Given this attitude toward your mate, it's no wonder that little irritations quickly erupt into full-blown explosions. If you find yourself prone to such a pattern, take a closer look. It's very likely that when you explode, you are expressing feelings about a number of issues, not just the one at hand. One woman I saw for a few years, Evelyn, always had a hard time talking to Will about what was bothering her. Throughout their ten years together, Will knew that once every few weeks some little thing he did—like forgetting to ask her about her day when he came home—would set her off. Then Evelyn would reel off an ever-expanding list of grievances that included everything from Will's "crazy" family to the smelly sneakers he had left in the foyer. In these moments, Will barely listened to Evelyn. Later, however, she began adding a few new charges—like "You don't really love me"—that were getting his attention.

People who continually miscommunicate and play charades with their partners invariably end up feeling unloved. And once you convince yourself that your partner does not love you, the incentive to change your style or work at a solution dies, along with your love.

Yes, it does take two to tango, but the fact is that men are not as comfortable expressing themselves as women are. There are many reasons for this. One is that men learn very early on that talking about their feelings indicates weakness and sometimes scares women away. Instead, they model their behavior on the false strength we characterize as typically male—not sharing anything and choosing to solve problems rather than discuss them. Women, on the other hand, talk about their feelings quite freely, sometimes too freely, and usually to the wrong people. They rarely ask directly for what they want and rarely take action to change a situation they are unhappy about. Neither approach ever leads to a solution.

Women equate talking with communicating. At the risk of sounding sexist, I will say that women generally do talk more than men do. Many times in my practice, I've listened as a woman has gone on and on about how her mate does not share himself emotionally with her. Meanwhile, he's sitting there waiting for a turn to talk. When I point out that she has not given him a chance to speak, she is usually embarrassed. Women are so used to being the communicators that they often don't even realize they're not giving their mate a chance to share.

## The Four Steps to Healthy Communication

Another lesson we need to learn is that not all communication is created equal. Some styles are simply better—more effective, more fair, more loving—than others. Again, the choice is yours. You can continue to express your feelings while making no promises of consequences, but that's called nagging or bitching, or you can find a better way.

Resolve to be a person who deserves respect, someone who means exactly what she says. Accept responsibility for your emotions, and express your feelings clearly. State what you want, ask for a commitment or a compromise, and follow through as you promised you would.

Remember Marcy, who had never told Gus how she felt about him? I'm happy to say that she began a new relationship, with a man named Martin. On the first date, she had a chance to practice her new skills. She was about to write him off because he had had too much to drink their first night out, but she bravely opted to speak up and try to handle the problem in an open, positive way instead. Following the Four Steps to Healthy Communication, Marcy said, "Martin, I felt upset that you drank so much on our first date. I want you to promise me that you won't do that again and that you will not have more than three drinks the next time we go out. Will you

## The Four Steps to
## Healthy Communication

We know that communication is important to every relationship, yet we do not always know how to communicate effectively. As you will see throughout this book, at the root of
every one of the Seven Dumbest Mistakes is a breakdown in
communication. Even when we think we have expressed ourselves, what we mean to say often gets lost in how we say it.
Speaking in vague, sweeping generalities, simply venting our
emotions, or just plain nagging does not work.

   To be sure that your partner understands you fully, make
a habit of voicing concerns in these four steps:

1. Express yourself: "I feel [*a specific emotion*] whenever you
   [*specify exactly what he does*]."
   Say how you feel, and identify who and what makes you
   feel that way. Own the feeling and be specific (do not say,
   "You make me so angry"), and don't attack (never say,
   "You're selfish"). Ideally, your communication would
   begin, "I feel angry when you ask me to change my plans
   to accommodate yours."
2. State what you want: "I want [*a specific behavior*]."
   When you state exactly what you want, you avoid the
   Dumb Mistake of expecting your mate to read your mind.
   Statements along the lines of "I want you to spend more
   time with me doing the things that I enjoy," "I want you
   to phone me when you think you will be late for dinner,"
   or "I want us to have sex more often" leave little room for
   argument and defuse the classic defense: "What do you
   want me to do about it?"
3. Ask for a commitment: "Will you [*give me what I want—
   be even more specific*]?"
   This is the only way to find out whether he has heard you
   and whether he intends to consider or comply with your
   request. "Will you spend more time going to places that
   I want to go, such as my office party next Friday night?"
   "Will you phone me next time you know you will be

late?" and "Will you have sex with me tonight?" are specific, to the point, and should yield a clear yes or no. If you get strong resistance or a halfhearted commitment—"I don't know if I can, but I'll try" then proceed to step 4.

4. Outline the consequences of your mate's reluctance or refusal to commit himself to change: "If not, I will [*state specifically what you will do*]."
This step tells him you are serious about your request. You might say, "If you won't spend more time with me doing things I like to do, I will make plans to spend that time with other people"; "If you don't call when you are late, I will assume you are not coming and will make other plans"; or "If you don't want to commit yourself to having a better sex life with me, I will leave this relationship and find someone else who does." If you really want to get what you want, you must have a plan to cover what you will do if you don't get it. If you don't follow the plan when the time comes, you will remain in the dependent role. This strategy strikes some women as needlessly aggressive, but this is because we are taught that if we present men with ultimatums, they will leave us. In fact, few of us ever put this doctrine to the test, and in failing to do so, we relinquish control over both our relationship and our lives. It's true—most people do react negatively to ultimatums; after all, no one likes to hear that there will be consequences for his or her next transgression. But issuing an ultimatum throws the ball into your mate's court and lets him know what you will do in response to his next play. At the very least, you make clear that you are holding him accountable for his behavior. In the process, you eliminate the fear of the unknown, since you know exactly what you will do the next time he behaves this way.

promise that? If not, I'm not comfortable going out with you again."

Because Marcy was direct, open, and nonjudgmental, because she took responsibility for her feelings and offered a clear alternative, Martin was not angry or offended. Marcy told Martin what she expected in a fashion that earned his respect and, happily, his cooperation. A year later they moved in together. But even if Marcy and Martin had ended up having only a brief, happy relationship, she would still have seen that instead of walking away when she didn't like a man's behavior, she could get him to treat her as she wished to be treated.

At times you may also have unresolved resentments to clean up in your relationship. You can use a modified version of

---

### Six Steps for Handling Past Resentments

1. "*I felt* very angry last Thanksgiving when you insisted that we travel a thousand miles to see your parents because, after all, we have spent every major holiday with them for the past four years."
2. "*I wanted* you to invite them to our house so that we could also spend time with my family that weekend."
3. "*Since you wouldn't* even discuss it, *I felt* that my desires and my feelings for my family were not considered as important as yours, and so I really resented the time I had to spend away from home with your family."
4. "*I should have* told you *then* how I really felt and insisted that we reach some kind of compromise. *If it happened now, I would* suggest that we work out some plan. I don't want this to continue to be an issue every year."
5. "*In the future,* let's try to come up with a better solution for handling this issue the next time it comes up."
6. "*If you refuse to negotiate, I will* stay here with my family next year."

the Four Steps to Healthy Communication to work through past resentments, as shown on page 82.

Try to put your resentment issues to rest with a plan for what each of you will do differently in the future. Finding resolution will save many future fights and act as a model for future negotiations.

## Roadblocks to Communication

### *We Don't Believe in Expressing Feelings Openly*

Like many women, Sarah assumed that because her husband, Brian, loved her, he would do whatever it took to have an emotionally intimate relationship with her. But she

---

**The New Beliefs
About Intimate Communication**

1. Men do not think the way women do. Men and women have different values and different styles of communicating and solving problems. Neither style is right or wrong, and neither he nor you can guess what each other wants.
2. Being strong means being able to take the risks necessary to express feelings and desires and actively seek solutions. It does not mean keeping your chin up and holding everything in.
3. It is healthy, not selfish, to be clear about, and ask for, what you want.
4. If you ask for what you want, you will probably get it.
5. Negative feelings that are not expressed or acted on will eventually poison the relationship.
6. Often a mate is eager to change his behavior and attitude if he sees a solution that will improve the relationship.

was wrong, and their marriage ended in divorce. A few years later, after reading my first book, Sarah came to see me because she recognized her role in damaging the marriage and wanted to try renewing her relationship with Brian. When she presented the idea to her ex, he told her that he still loved her, and he agreed to try again, with the help of marriage counseling.

Brian was initially cooperative in therapy and was even overly agreeable in their negotiations about money, their children, and their respective work schedules. But he soon made clear that he didn't like having to talk about and analyze their relationship. Each time he was asked to share his feelings, he would respond by asking, "Can't we just let bygones be bygones? What does the past have to do with now, anyway?" Brian was unconvinced when I explained how his and Sarah's past problems would recur if they didn't both express their feelings and seek new solutions to their old issues. Instead, he begged Sarah to let him move back in with her and urged that they get on with their lives, without this "stupid" counseling. When Sarah insisted they continue the counseling, Brian became increasingly abusive, just as he had been in the marriage. He tried to intimidate Sarah by telling her she was stupid to let counseling "run our lives."

If Brian really did love Sarah, why was he so adamantly opposed to making the changes that might have rekindled her love for him? When we tried to question his resistance to opening up, Brian denied having any negative feelings. Had he admitted to feeling angry, he would have been admitting that Sarah had hurt him. Instead, he tried to pretend he was too strong to let that happen. "Besides," he told me, "Sarah knows what she's done wrong in this relationship. I don't have to tell her." Once I had Sarah out of the room, he admitted to feeling irritation about some small things, but he saw no reason to upset her by bringing them up. He had convinced himself that he felt no anger, and he believed that whatever irritation he might have felt was unimportant.

Like many people, Brian could not see how clearly his feelings were showing even when he did not intend them to. Sarah told me that she was acutely aware of how Brian felt toward her, but she could never understand *why* he was upset since he wouldn't talk about it. She could feel his rage in the disrespectful, condescending, and chauvinistic way he talked to her. In choosing to fight with her over relatively minor, ridiculous issues and making her guess what he was thinking, Brian revealed more than he imagined yet gave Sarah no information she could use to solve the problems. When I confronted Brian about this, he became extremely defensive; he said that this was all "too much work" and if two people really loved each other, they shouldn't have to work so hard.

Brian's real problem was that he had no understanding of what an emotionally intimate relationship requires. He was not willing to share his innermost feelings or figure out why he believed and acted as he did. In refusing to do this, Brian made clear that any future relationship between him and Sarah would be on his terms, terms Sarah now realized were unacceptable to her. Given what she knew now, she could never go back to the way things were before, with Brian doing pretty much as he pleased, Sarah playing the obedient wife and mom, and neither of them ever talking about how they really felt.

Of course, Sarah was crushed when she realized she had no future with Brian. Eventually, however, she saw that it was Brian's inability to be intimate that killed their relationship, not his lack of love or anything that was wrong with her. Finally, she was able to walk away and seek a mate who shared her desire for intimacy.

One of the messages we assimilate as children is that strong people control their emotions and refuse to be affected by them. Many of us admire people who act tough and unemotional, and we may choose to emulate them because they seem impervious to the hurt and pain we sometimes feel.

Often these people are so good at maintaining their façade—or we are so willing to believe in it—that we conclude, erroneously, that they are stronger than we are. The truth is that people who withhold and fail to admit to or process their emotions suffer from psychological and physical stress. Studies show that unexpressed emotion, anger in particular, can cause illness and premature death.

We know that fully sharing our emotions makes us vulnerable. Think of some of the slogans we live by—"Never let them see you sweat," "Grin and bear it," "Big girls don't cry." Whereas in certain situations—at work, for example—this advice may well be the best, in the context of a deep, loving relationship, it is seldom appropriate.

### We Edit Our Feelings Because We Believe Our Mate Can't Handle Them

The common belief that our mate can't handle our feelings arises from several underlying attitudes toward love. One of these is that everything about love should be happy and easy. When you hold this attitude, you leave no room for conflict or disagreement; the very suggestion that either of you might feel unhappiness or anger is extremely threatening to you. Another underlying attitude about love is that negative emotions are inappropriate when you love someone—that there is something bad, wrong, or out of control about expressing anger or unhappiness to someone you love. All of us—but women in particular—are taught not to hurt people we love, not to say mean things, not to lash out in anger.

No one enjoys confrontations with loved ones, but they are necessary to a healthy, strong, intimate relationship. No matter how we disguise it with noble motives, the more traditional approach requires that we be emotionally dishonest with our mate and with ourselves. We may "protect" our mate from the pain of our unhappiness, but sooner or later even we do not really buy what we've been telling ourselves and him.

Perhaps even more detrimental than protecting his feelings is the distance we create within ourselves. Editing our part of our conversations with our mate leaves us starved for substantive, honest communication. While we may rationalize our reason for choosing not to share our real feelings, deep inside we know the truth. There is no satisfaction in telling somebody what he wants to hear, nothing ennobling about "protecting" our mate from ourselves.

When we edit ourselves, we begin to lose ourselves. Blocking our negative feelings is risky because it leaves us unsure of whether we're the person who felt that emotion or another person who is trying not to feel it. If we keep denying who we are and how we feel, before long we will not know what to think or feel. Besides, when we get this far out of touch with ourselves, there's no personality left for our mate to bond with.

Feelings are like energy: They can assume different forms, but they can never be destroyed. Despite their great number and variety, all our emotions are wired into one switch, and either it's on or it's off. It is impossible to block selectively one kind of emotion or all emotions directed toward one person without shutting down or contaminating the whole circuit. When we feel something negative toward our mate and choose not to express it, we taint all our emotions toward him, including our positive, loving feelings. Eventually, some of us, especially men, lose the ability to feel anything—anger, sadness, or joy—and become emotionally dead.

A client, thirty-two-year-old Jody, came to see me because she felt herself emotionally separating from her husband, Ross. She said that she loved him very much but always felt angry with him. When I asked her what she was angry about, she replied that it was "nothing in particular, just a lot of little things." As we talked, it became clear that all those "little things"—such as Ross's never being home to see their sons play soccer and his being too exhausted to do anything fun with her—stemmed from the long hours he put in at work. As the vice president of sales for a booming national chain of coffeehouses, Ross was earning a great salary, but he was rarely home.

Though Jody said she wanted more time alone with Ross, whenever they were together, she ruined it with her constant nagging and complaining. For example, when he surprised her by arranging a second honeymoon in New York City, Jody found fault with almost everything, from the Plaza Hotel's room service to the hit play Ross got front-row tickets for. She didn't seem interested in Ross or anything he said or wanted to do. The silent car ride home was punctuated by Jody's sarcastic observations. Ross seldom even tried anymore because he had begun to emotionally shut down. Exasperated, Ross finally said, "I don't know what on earth you want. We never get to be alone together, and then when we are, I can't seem to ever please you. I don't know why I even bother."

"How would I know?" Jody replied sarcastically, her voice rising in anger. "You're never here. Then when you are, you expect me to think everything you do is so great!"

Jody had been holding back her anger about Ross's schedule because she truly enjoyed the financial benefits of his position. "I know how lucky we are that Ross has this great job," Jody said, rationalizing her feelings. "After all, virtually all of my friends have to work full-time. At least I'm home for the kids, so I suppose I shouldn't complain."

Like many of us, Jody was able to avoid expressing her emotions directly, but she did not stop feeling them—instead she built resentment. And, further, she could not harbor unexpressed anger toward Ross and still feel loving toward him.

No one ever taught us that there is a positive, effective way to express anger and hurt. Instead, we were taught the impossible, no-win option of ignoring the issues altogether, as Jody did, which builds resentment. Of course, it's impossible to continue ignoring them, and so when the anger and hurt reach their critical mass, we do one of the only two things we ever learned to do: leave or explode. When we are faced with only these two options, it's no wonder we fear expressing ourselves. We are truly afraid that we will lose control, say things we will regret, and ruin our relationship *simply because* we communicated our unhappiness. If, however, we address our concerns on a case-by-case basis, as they occur, following the Four Steps to Healthy Communication, this should not happen.

## We Think Telling Him Won't Do Any Good

You probably cannot count the number of times you have been told, "Don't think you'll change him. You won't." And it's true: You cannot change another person's basic disposition or belief system. What you can change, however, is the way in which your mate treats you, but to do that, you have to set boundaries and take risks. One reason most of us have trouble doing this is that we have so rarely seen it work for other people. Avoiding confrontation seems like a good idea since the truth seems only to make people defensive and unwilling to deal with the issue at hand. Perhaps we fear confrontation because most confrontations we have seen involve pent-up anger and aging grievances on one side and surprise on the other.

The sooner in the relationship you express your likes and your dislikes, what you consider acceptable and what you consider unacceptable, the greater the chance you will influence his behavior toward you. Ever since Jody met Ross, fifteen years ago, she always worked her schedule around his; one year they even celebrated Thanksgiving a week late because he was away on business. For years, Jody never complained; in fact, she let him know how much she appreciated his hard work and the money he earned. No wonder Ross didn't see anything wrong with putting in such long hours and couldn't understand why she always seemed angry with him.

We so rarely encounter people whose words jibe with their actions that we habitually disregard what everyone says most of the time. We have learned since childhood to judge what people really mean by what they do. That's why if you pretend to ignore your mate's insults, for instance, your actions will send the message that you are strong enough to handle them, and he will conclude that his behavior is acceptable to you. When you finally speak up, he will be entitled to feel that you have been less than honest with him before or that you have suddenly changed the rules. At that point, your mate is focused on why you never mentioned your feelings before, not on what you want him to do now.

### We Push Our Mate Away Through Criticism and Sarcasm

One of the hardest things for us to do is openly admit to and express our hurt, anger, or disappointment, so instead we resort to such forms of indirect and unhealthy communication as whining, arguing, judging, ordering, advising, moralizing, and withdrawing. The barb, the judgmental remark, the sarcastic aside—all give us the illusion we are really expressing ourselves from a position of strength. Because we are not revealing how hurt we truly feel, we feel somewhat protected.

You may say that you want your mate to know how you feel and to do something about it, but the fact is that when you choose to communicate indirectly, you ensure that he will not be able to respond in a constructive, reasoned manner. After all, remarks like "You're so inconsiderate," "I might as well talk to the wall," and "It's all your fault" are attacks, and attacks demand defense. Under these circumstances, anyone would be a fool to open himself up emotionally. By communicating like this, you have served notice that you intend to keep your mate at bay and will focus on what he did wrong rather than on what the two of you might do to fix the problem. He ends up feeling continually punished. Would you feel comfortable opening up to someone who treated you like that?

## We Get Release by Telling Someone Else What We Should Be Telling Our Mate

One reason we long for true intimacy is that we know talking about our problems often makes us feel better. And for the most part, we are correct. Voicing our emotions does provide some relief, and the commiseration of our friends can comfort, reassure, and sometimes vindicate us. The classic situation is the girlfriend who knows everything *he's* ever done to you, but *he* doesn't know it. For example, whenever Ross was out of town on business, Jody would call her best friend, Peggy, and complain about him. She would begin the conversation feeling intensely angry, but after Peggy's commiseration, Jody always felt much better. She had not expressed her feelings to Ross, and she and Ross were no closer to a resolution, but for Jody just feeling better was enough. It took the edge off her anger and delayed her next blowup with Ross. Unfortunately, it also contributed to the emotional distance between them.

In creating good relationships, our emotions are the most elemental resources. Feelings are like bricks—they can form bridges or they can form walls; it all depends on how you use them. When you share your feelings and thoughts with your mate, you build a bridge, a bond, between you. When you choose instead to vent your feelings about him to others, you build walls. There's nothing wrong with discussing your problems with a trusted friend or a loved one—as long as you use that communication to support yourself when you do talk to your mate and not as a means to avoid talking to him.

There are three other risks you take when you bad-mouth the man in your life. The first is that your relationship might subsequently change for the better or you may realize later that you blew things out of proportion. By then, you may have so thoroughly demonized him that your friends will try to dissuade you from continuing the relationship and may never come around to liking him. Since most of us, when we tell our side of a story, pretty much stick to our side (that is, we don't fully reveal how we caused or contributed to the problem), we often recruit friends to our cause. Unfortunately, no matter how things improve between you and your mate, your friends will tend to remain loyal to the cause. If it was seeing him as a jerk, you can be pretty sure your friends will continue to see him that way.

The second risk is that in discussing your mate with someone else, you will forge a deeper emotional bond with that person than you have with your mate. If that person is of the opposite sex, this instant—though partial—emotional intimacy could well open the door to an affair.

The third risk is that the person you talk to most likely still ascribes to the false beliefs and values that you are—or should be—trying to break away from. Her or his advice, however well intended, may send you back to the very behavior patterns you are trying to break out of.

Sharing secrets builds bonds. When you share private information about your mate and your relationship with others, you invite them into the relationship, which can be undesirable, even dangerous. How would you feel knowing that your mate had discussed intimate details about you and cast you in an unflattering light? This is not to say that you should never discuss your problems with confidants and loved ones, only that you should do so selectively and with your eyes open. Are you really talking about your problems or just whining about him? Are you truly seeking helpful advice and insight, or are you recruiting supporters for your cause? Does your talking about your problems make it easier for you to then discuss them with him, or does it leave you feeling better about saying nothing to him? Here's the rule: Never tell anyone anything about your mate that you have not already told him. The only exception is when you have decided to tell him something and are discussing it with someone as a way to prepare.

### We Want to Be Chased Emotionally

*If he really loved me, he would know something was wrong,* Jody told herself again and again. *He should try harder to find out what's bothering me.* How many times have you thought this? There is nothing wrong with fantasizing about the lover who is so acutely attuned to your feelings that with just one look, he will know what you want. Just remember, this man does not exist. He would have to continually ask, "Are you OK, honey? Is it something I did? How can I help you?" It is humanly impossible for anyone to always know what another is thinking or feeling. Think of how many times you have assumed that your mate felt one way or another and later you discovered you were wrong. And wordless communication is easily misread. While you assume your moodiness is inviting him to ask you what's wrong, he is probably interpreting it as your way of saying you need your space. Or when you storm around the house and he asks you what's wrong and you reply, "Nothing," don't blame him if he takes you at your (dishonest) word.

## How to Communicate Successfully

### Don't Avoid, or Talk Yourself Out of, Your Feelings

When faced with difficulty, often our first response is to avoid it altogether. Jody often denied her anger by reminding herself, *Ross works so hard, and we have such a beautiful home. What am I complaining about? It's not that bad.* Unfortunately, we have been raised to equate having a problem with being a failure. Instead, we must begin to view each problem as an opportunity to improve our relationship, learn more about ourselves and our mate, and perhaps even discover ways to love him even more. When you and your mate face and work through your problems together, you strengthen the bond between you and increase the likelihood that you will weather the next challenge (and there will be one) successfully.

### Make Statements, Not Judgments

When two people become a couple, they often start believing that they should feel and think the same way about everything. You do have the right to tell your mate how you feel about what he is doing. But you have no right to make him feel like a bad person for doing it. Admittedly, this is not always easy, especially in the heat of anger. One way to retrain yourself is to replace any statement beginning with "you" with one beginning with "I." For instance, say, "I feel very lonely when you go out with your friends every Friday night," not "You shouldn't want to be with your friends instead of me." Or say, "I feel hurt when you tell me you are angry," not "You have no right to be angry with me." (See the chart on page 95 for more examples.)

### Admit Your Part to Your Mate

Admit that you've expected your mate to read your mind and that it wasn't fair to do so. Admit that you wanted him to chase you emotionally and that you may have been wanting him to compensate for the affection or acceptance you believe you didn't get from someone else earlier in your life. Admit that you've been afraid to tell him what you want and how you really feel. Then let him know what sets off your reactions and why.

| Unhealthy Communication Style | Don't Say . . . | Say . . . |
| --- | --- | --- |
| Judgmental | "You should be nicer to my friends." | "It hurts me when you treat my friends as if you don't like them." |
| Argumentative | "You know that's a lie." "You're wrong!" | "I know you believe that to be true, but I don't agree, and here's why." |
| Whiny | "You never want to do what I want to do." | "I would like you to do more things with me, but if you won't, I'll go out with my friends instead." |
| Authoritative | "Stop watching TV and come talk to me!" | "I feel lonely and want you to talk to me." |
| Advisory | "You need to tell your boss not to treat you like that." | "Would you like my advice?" [If he answers yes, tell him how you would—as opposed to how he should—handle the situation.] |
| Sarcastic | "OK, Magellan, how many hundreds of miles off course are we now?" | "I think we would get there sooner if we stopped and asked for directions." |
| Moralistic | "It's wrong to look at other women when you're married." | "I feel uncomfortable when you blatantly stare at other women when we're together." |
| Analytical | "It's obvious that you're treating me the same way you treated your mother." | "All of that anger is not about me. Who or what are you really mad about?" |
| Critical | "Why did you send me a dozen yellow roses? You know I hate yellow." | "Thank you for the beautiful flowers. Yellow roses are cheery, but I like red ones, too, because they're so romantic." |

## Be Vulnerable Yet Strong

The driving emotion behind anger is always hurt. Unfortunately, we are so conditioned to equate anger with hostility that we do not think of an angry person as someone in pain. That is why we usually respond defensively at first and do not really hear what the angry person is trying to say. If your communication begins with an expression of vulnerability, you will have a better chance of working things out. Always begin with "I"—not "you" or "men"—and state your feelings, not an opinion of your mate or the situation. Statements that begin "I'm hurt," "I'm sad," "I feel rejected and unloved," "I'm depressed," "I feel guilty," "I'm worried," or "I'm sorry" are invitations, not accusations. When we are vulnerable in a healthy way, those we love tend to move toward, rather than away from, us. From that point, you can follow the Four Steps to Healthy Communication.

If, on the other hand, your mate verbally attacks you in spite of your vulnerability, you can and should defend your boundary. Get angry. Be strong and definite, and have a plan. You might say, "I'm trying to share something with you, but if you don't want to listen and work it out, then I'm not talking to you. I am not going to let you treat me this way." Then pull away from him until he begins to hear you.

## Learn to Emotionally Process

It is difficult to tell your mate what you feel unless you have taken the time to check in with yourself and truly know. Since we are never taught to do this, we rarely consider how we feel until a serious crisis leaves us no choice. Then we may end up regretting what we say or how we say it. By then, however, it is usually too late to save the relationship anyway. (This, by the way, is where we get the idea that communicating doesn't work.) Jody knew she felt angry toward Ross, but because she hadn't taken the time to pinpoint what was bothering her, she could not effectively express herself to him or begin working toward solutions.

Having emotional depth and the ability to share ourselves with a mate comes from understanding ourselves, yesterday and today. People often ask, "Why do we have to dwell on the past?" I always tell them that the process of examining your life is not about "dwelling" or "staying stuck" in the past. The real goal is to correlate, to see the connections between what happened before and what is happening now. Recognizing and understanding these relationships is like finding a map to buried treasure. For every problem you face, there are probably dozens of possible solutions, but until you understand yourself and why you feel as you do, the right solution—the one that will work for you—will remain a mystery.

When we go back and process old issues, we don't just talk about them. We really let ourselves feel, and then we act on what we have learned. Simply making the intellectual decision to change something does not make it magically happen. Imagine how simple life would be if that were all we had to do. Emotional processing works because emotions are extremely strong motivators, far stronger than reason or intelligence. The difference between truly processing your emotions and simply talking about your past is like the difference between experiencing a balloon ride and talking about going on one.

When we keep in touch with ourselves and connect emotionally to our past, we find it much easier to become emotionally engaged in the present. The way to get in touch—and stay in touch—with your feelings is to get into the habit of periodically (say, every few days, or on laundry day, or while you're driving home for the weekend) asking yourself, *How do I feel right now? If I'm upset, whom am I upset with? What do I want to see happen instead? What can I do to make that happen? What am I willing to do if he doesn't come through for me?*

After a few months of therapy, Jody realized she was being unfair to herself, to Ross, and to their relationship. She carefully thought through what she was angry about and considered several possible compromises she and Ross could try. One day, Jody told Ross, "I have been feeling very angry for quite a while because your work has taken you away from our family and from me. I want you to work with me to figure out some way that you can either cut back your hours at work or, if that's impossible, make our time together and with the kids more fun."

Ross, who was beginning to wonder whether Jody even loved him anymore, was relieved to hear that she was really angry about the hours he worked, not the clothes he chose, how he spoke to the kids, the way he chopped lettuce, or any of a hundred little things she'd been picking on him about. Together they reached a compromise: Ross would arrange for a junior executive to attend out-of-town meetings whenever possible, and Jody would switch the boys into a soccer league that played on Saturdays instead of Fridays so Ross could see their games. Because Ross never had business commitments on Sundays, they designated Sunday night their special date night. And they also agreed that anytime Ross's business took him to an exciting city during school vacations, they would make it a family trip, even if only for the weekend.

### Reveal Your True Self

Without revealing your true personality—flaws included—you will never expose enough of yourself for someone to truly love and grow attached to you. You will never enjoy an intense, deep bond if all you present of yourself is the edited version. In the drive to present the most acceptable face, we often unknowingly leave out those aspects of our personality and our life that are the most interesting, the ones that better illuminate who we are. When Alan and I first got together, he could see that I had a controlling attitude at times. It was not one of

---

### How to Process Your Emotions

1. Admit that something in your life is not working the way you want it to.
2. Admit to the emotion you feel about this problem. For example, *This depresses/angers/upsets me.*
3. Allow yourself to feel the pain fully; then find out when in your past you felt this way before and why. Ask yourself whether there is a pattern, whether this is something you have felt with other mates or your parents.
4. Decide what you want. Let both your intellect and your emotions guide you to find a solution that involves both your head and your heart.
5. Visualize yourself handling the problem with your mate using the Four Steps to Healthy Communication.
6. Act on your decision.

---

my more lovable characteristics, but Alan found it easier to live with after I told him about my past. As I explained, I controlled because I was good at it, and I was good at it because for as far back as my teens, my family had given me ample opportunity to perfect it. Now, years later, controlling Alan was more a finely developed habit than a malicious act directed toward him personally. Of course, none of this excused me, and I worked very hard to monitor and change my behavior. But knowing this also gave Alan greater insight. He knew it was not "about" him, and this knowledge made it easier for him to disengage himself from the behavior. It also gave him another part of me to learn about and to love.

### Learn to Fight Fair

Couples often fight dirty without knowing it. Dirty fighting usually has long-term negative effects on the relationship.

## How to Fight Fair

- *When listening to him, force yourself to repeat to him the feeling and content of what he said,* to be sure you understood it, *before* you respond or move on to your next point. For example, say, "I hear you saying that you are angry with me because I always take phone calls, even when they come in the middle of a romantic dinner."

- *Allow yourself and/or your mate to take time-outs when fighting,* especially if one of you feels tired, or has been drinking, or both of you agree that all you are doing is treading old ground. But do this only if you both promise to resume the discussion at a later date and commit yourselves to resolving the issue.

- *Develop neutral code words or phrases to stop fights or to let your mate know he's going too far.* Sometimes a gesture works well, too. One couple I know press their fingers together in a particular way and say, "Moose truce!"

- *Agree that certain forms of expression are unacceptable*— for instance, name-calling, damaging property, physical intimidation (pushing, shoving). If one of you does this, the other has the right to withdraw.

- *Be specific and factual.* When talking about your mate, you may want to say, "He always . . ." and "He never . . ." While the aspects of his behavior you're complaining about might apply in some instances, they rarely apply every time or never. That's not to say that the 50 percent of the time when he shows up late doesn't make you feel as if he's never on time. It probably does, and the complaint is valid. Managers in business are taught that the golden rule of discussing problems with staff members is to be specific. Angrily shouting "You are always late, and I've had it!" is self-defeating and begs to be challenged with "I am not always late, and you know it." Discussions like this quickly run in circles and produce nothing but more anger and more misunderstanding.

- *Give complaints an expiration date.* Once you have cleaned up an issue, give complaints about it an expiration date. No one can change the past, and while you can hold someone responsible for his past behavior, bringing it up after you've resolved the issue is punishing and makes him feel defensive.

## Model the Kind of Communication You Want from Him

Chances are one of you may not be as enthusiastic about adopting a new way of communicating as the other, or you may not be as willing or able to do it. In the heat of the moment, it's not always easy to stick to the Four Steps to Healthy Communication. Just don't let his poor communication skills justify yours. If you really want to change the communication style of your relationship, you must model the style you aspire to. Simply by speaking clearly, openly, and honestly, you can often defuse an angry situation. At the very least, you will not have contributed to its escalation and the resulting resentment and misunderstanding.

## Confront Your Mate About Sharing Himself with You

If you're living with a noncommunicator, don't be afraid to confront your mate about his or her attitude toward communication. Following the Four Steps to Healthy Communication, you might say something like this:

> "*I feel* frustrated *when you refuse* to do what's necessary to work on our problems.
> "*I want* you to tell me what's wrong, and if you don't know, then I need you to get some help to figure it out.
> "*Will you* try to talk to me or make an appointment with a therapist or do whatever is necessary to figure this out?

*"If not, I will not* continue to try to do this alone. I will pull away from you and do whatever is necessary to take care of my own needs."

Be sure that you tell him what you are doing and why; then let him know that the next move is his. Invite him to let you know when he's ready to deal with this. Then—and I know this is the hard part—do not bring it up again. Pull away and get busy with friends, hobbies, and other interests. Remember, following through with step 4 in the Four Steps to Healthy Communication is crucial. When you don't follow through, you send the message that you did not really mean what you said in the first three steps.

### Create an Atmosphere That Fosters Mutual Emotional Participation

From my practice and my personal life, I can tell you that people can and do change, no matter what their relationship history. For example, Alan and I discussed from the start the kind of relationship we wanted to have: equal and intimate. The problem was how to achieve that. Alan, like Sarah's ex-husband, Brian, did not really believe in sharing feelings. He had not done much of it during a seventeen-year marriage, and when I met him, he proudly described himself as a "very discreet person." Initially, I was much more open than Alan, but a few months into our relationship I realized that we were not sharing equally. I made a conscious decision to be less open until Alan began contributing his feelings and told him of my decision. Since closing up went against my nature, it did take some effort to pull back, but I knew that setting the right course from the start was easier than trying to fix things later. My pulling back forced Alan to contribute to the intimacy, and he did.

It is important to remember that when we speak of "forcing" someone to share or of "pulling back" from him, we are making a value judgment not of that person but of the bad lessons he has picked up and practiced to perfection up until now. Had I continued creating intimacy by sharing my feelings without demanding that Alan reciprocate, he probably would not have changed—not because he is a bad person but because that is all he (and most of us) ever knew.

Alan and I learned that in order to have an intimate relationship, we had to contribute to it equally and continually. It took forethought and effort, and it didn't happen overnight. But we believed then that the emotional investment we were making at that time would yield dividends in the future, and it has. It is easier to address problems and express ourselves sooner rather than later. We know from past experience that we're committed to working things through. And we have seen that any problem in the relationship can have a silver lining if we view its solution as an opportunity to strengthen our bond.

# 5

# Mistake Number Three:
# Playing the Martyr

As we all learned in school, martyrs are individuals who willingly sacrifice their lives for a higher purpose. Great works of history, literature, and religion promote the martyr as an ideal, a role to which we should all aspire. In real life, however, everyday martyrs are people—often, but not always, women—who sacrifice their personality, dreams, ambition, self-esteem, and true desires in the name of love. We often end up playing the martyr because we know of no other way of dealing with someone we love. Martyrdom flourishes in the darkness of unspoken thoughts and feelings, unresolved conflicts, and unprotected boundaries. It yields a bumper crop of resentment, anger, disappointment, and self-hatred, and wherever it takes root, it poisons love.

You may be playing the martyr if you find yourself routinely engaging in any of the following behaviors:

- *Making sacrifices.* Do you rarely say no and usually agree to do things for your mate even though you know you will resent it later? Do you go along to get along, choosing not to disagree or argue with your mate even if doing so goes against your true feelings? Do you do whatever he wants you to do even if it is harmful to you? Do you allow him to use you sexually even if he disregards your needs or you are not feeling close to each other?

- *Depending on your mate for your happiness.* Do you think, *I would be happy if only he loved me more/would stop drinking/made more money,* and so on? Do you hand over to him responsibility for certain aspects of your life? Do you isolate yourself from friends and family members because he doesn't like them? Do you ask him for constant reassurance that you are good enough? When he puts you down, discounts you, or behaves condescendingly toward you, do you think it's because you deserve it?

- *Putting your mate on a pedestal.* Do you believe he is braver, stronger, or better than you are? Do you remain loyal to your mate even after he hurts you? Do you always try to understand and forgive? Do you alternate between idealizing and devaluing your mate, one moment praising him, the next moment putting him down? When your mate attacks you, do you first pause and question yourself rather than question him? Do you let your mate make most of the decisions in your relationship because you believe he knows more than you do?

- *Cowering when attacked.* Do you whine, nag, and complain about him yet never stand up to him? Do you make excuses to yourself and others for your mate's bad behavior? After a fight or a breakup, do you desperately promise to change and apologize to him to save the relationship even when you know you were not at fault?

- *Resorting to passive-aggressive behavior.* Instead of expressing your anger directly, do you overdraw the checking account, forget to give him important phone messages, promise to do things and then fail to follow through, or sabotage him in some other way?

If you answered yes to any of these questions, you are probably playing the martyr. When you engage in this behavior, you allow and even encourage your mate to behave badly toward you. Whether this behavior entails his being chronically late or physically battering you, the underlying causes are the same. Like forcing intimacy and expecting your mate to read your mind, playing the martyr begins when you choose to accept and live by false values and beliefs that are detrimental to your personal emotional health and to the stability of your relationship. In fact, you can view embracing martyrdom as just a few steps further in a progression that begins with forcing intimacy and expecting your mate to read your mind. As you will see in the cases discussed here, martyrdom usually begins with the woman making one or both of those mistakes.

## Why Martyrdom Looks Better Than It Is

Unfortunately, we are raised to believe that there is something grand and noble about martyrdom, selflessness, and sacrifice. The heroine of the story is always the one who puts the good, the safety, and the happiness of others before her own. Our definition of a good mother includes a catalog of self-effacing, self-denying behaviors. The so-called good wife stands silently in her mate's shadow and yields her interests to his and to their children's.

People who behave in these ways are "good," and they usually know it. So do others. More than a century ago the English nurse Florence Nightingale wrote, "The martyr sacrifices herself entirely in vain. Or rather not in vain; for she makes the selfish more selfish, the lazy more lazy, the narrow narrower." When we play the martyr, we make ourselves eternal givers in a world of takers. Takers instinctively seek out mates who will give, so again, opposites do attract in a dysfunctional controller/dependent way.

There is nothing inherently wrong with doing things for those we love, with making sacrifices and putting others ahead of us when the situation warrants it. In a healthy, balanced relationship, our sacrifices and gifts are compromises matched by our mate's. The act of giving is one expression of our love, not the dominant aspect of our personality. It should be recognized and appreciated, not expected. For women who play the martyr, however, this kind of behavior eventually becomes an automatic response to every potential conflict. There are several erroneous beliefs that lead us into and help us sustain this kind of behavior, but the most compelling one is that men prefer to dominate us and that our going along with their domination makes them appreciate us. After all, we're not making demands or causing trouble. As a parent loves a good child, they should love us even more, right?

Wrong. Even men who take advantage of women in this way lose respect for them sooner or later. In the end, the partner learns that all her sacrifice was for naught. She crawls out of the relationship months, years, even decades later with nothing to show for it, least of all her self-esteem.

Helen and Bruce were in their late twenties and had been married three years. Helen initially came in to see me because she was very depressed. She had worked as a sales representative for a national cosmetics company until Bruce forced her to quit because he said, "My wife doesn't work." For the first year or so, she busied herself decorating their new home. When she told Bruce she had nothing to do, he suggested she help his ailing parents. Helen obliged. As the eldest of six, she had been taught that loving someone demands sacrifice and that only bad and weak people complain.

Now, two years later, Helen was driving Bruce's father to doctor's appointments at least once and sometimes two or three times a week, doing his parents' grocery shopping, and cleaning their house. When Bruce got home at night, he expected dinner on the table, fresh linens on the bed, and a six-pack cooling in the refrigerator. If things were not to his liking, he launched into a recap of everything Helen had done wrong since the day they met. But she did not stand up to Bruce or stop taking care of everything. Every weekend, Helen drove her in-laws to visit their other children and their grandchildren while Bruce played in his softball league, worked out at the gym, or hung out with his buddies at the local sports bar.

After several therapy sessions, Helen dragged Bruce to my office. When I asked him whether he realized that he was controlling, even abusing, his wife, he denied that his behavior was abusive, and replied, "I know I asked her to do lots of things for my folks, but she didn't mind. After all, she did it and never asked me to help instead of hanging out with my friends. Besides, she knows she's got a good deal and I know that no matter how bad it gets, she isn't going to leave."

Bruce's point reminds me of the rationalization we hear from people who demand exorbitant prices for worthless junk: "Well, if they're dumb enough to pay for it, why shouldn't I charge that much?" Why not, indeed?

I can hear you saying, "What do you mean, why not? Well, because it is wrong, unfair, unjust, and bad to treat people like that." And you are right. A woman in a healthy relationship may believe that, too, but she recognizes that life is unfair and gives herself the responsibility and permission to create her own justice when others or "the world" refuses. In contrast, a martyr like Helen persists in believing that justice will eventually prevail and that her sacrifices will pay off. When they don't, instead of changing her behavior, she tries harder, thinking she didn't do it right the first time. Her first and biggest mistake is handing over to someone else—namely, the person whose love she is making sacrifices for—the power and then waiting for her sacrificing to pay off. Her next mistake is not knowing when to stop giving to him.

Kelly was the classic superwoman. She raised two kids, cooked, cleaned, and catered to her husband's every need. When he complained about the household's finances, she launched a successful computer-graphics business. Kelly believed that keeping her family happy would make her happy. She first came to see me after she learned that her husband, Greg, was having an affair. By then, he had moved out of the house and was dating the new woman openly.

Kelly was devastated, and she vowed to win him back. Instead of feeling angry with Greg and getting over him, she asked me to tell her what to do to keep him and make him love her. Any time he snapped his fingers, she would run over to his house and have sex with him. She let him trample over her personal boundaries in virtually every area of her life. She made herself available to Greg and refused to hold him accountable in any way because she believed that by being a good person, she could make him love her again.

The longer she waited for Greg to return, the more desperate Kelly became. She resented him, but the more he pushed her away, the more determined she was to reclaim him. Depressed, at times even suicidal, Kelly just could not envision life without Greg. She was at a loss as to how to take charge and create a life for herself without him. She felt she could never be happy unless he returned to her. This was interesting because when I asked her why she wanted him back so badly, she admitted that she didn't know, since she was not really that happy in the marriage, merely content.

Kelly adamantly refused to see the writing on the wall until I suggested she bring Greg to my office. There Greg clearly told Kelly that he did not want a relationship with her any longer. He also said that while he enjoyed having sex with her once in a while, they would never again be a couple. Only then did Kelly get angry about how he had treated her throughout the marriage. She started setting limits with Greg. He was upset when she first refused his phone calls and made herself unavailable for sex. After all, he had been eating his cake and having it, too. It took a lot of work for Kelly to stop being a martyr, but she has since built a new life of her own.

## Why It's So Easy to Tolerate Bad Behavior

### *We Don't Want to Take Charge of Our Lives, and We Think We Shouldn't Have To*

Women who embrace martyrdom and permit unacceptable behavior continually complain, "Why would he do that to me? I can't imagine treating anyone that way!" Naïvely, we expect others to live by the values we live by. We confuse wishing we lived in a peaceful, caring world with believing that we actually do.

Choosing to see things as they ought to be rather than as they are is dangerous. It leads us to the wrong conclusions, so we make bad decisions. It distracts us from the real issues, so we continue to repeat mistakes without ever solving the real problem. It encourages us to abdicate responsibility for ourselves and for ensuring the quality of our relationships, so we give our mate free rein. And when things go wrong, it often paralyzes us so that we fail to take the appropriate action. When we believe there is nothing we can or should do to protect ourselves (because things just happen, or he's just that way, or that's just life), we leave ourselves open to a host of bad behaviors, ranging from verbal abuse to violent assault.

### *We Think Control and Abuse in Love Is Normal*

Without realizing it or understanding why, we sometimes choose a mate who treats us exactly as our parents treated us. If we are fortunate enough to have grown up in a healthy, warm environment, we will be drawn naturally to relationships that re-create that emotional climate. But if our parents

were critical, unavailable, or scolding, for example, those behaviors will become part of our definition of love, and we will
seek relationships with people who treat us the same way.
When parents behave in ways that make us feel unhappy, insecure, or fearful, then tell us, "I wouldn't do that if I didn't
love you," we may grow up believing that we need and
deserve abuse or punishment to keep us in line, to keep us
lovable. Unfortunately, this dynamic typifies many fathers' relationships with their wives and children, and you probably
come from a home where some degree of control occurred,
so you may consider "being controlled" normal. This control
may have been as simple as your father yelling at you about
not doing your homework or criticizing your mother for her
weight. In any case, it's important to remember that normal
is not the same as healthy.

Remember Helen, who took care of Bruce's parents in
spite of his verbal abuse? Initially, Helen did not see how
Bruce abused her. This was because all her life she had been
yelled at, humiliated, and punished by people who loved her
(like her parents) and people who, she was told, were doing
these things for her own good (the teachers at her parochial
school). As I told Helen, the best way to change your thinking is to concentrate emotionally on how these controlling situations make you feel. Period. Stop yourself before you say
"but" and give the controller an excuse. For example, in discussing her childhood, Helen would say, "Sure, my mother
yelled all the time, but I know she loved me," or "Yes, they
did hit us a lot in parochial school, but they gave us the best
education I could have gotten." If you look closely at these
statements, you will see that they are almost non sequiturs.
One day I said to Helen, "I want you to think about something: What does yelling have to do with love, or corporal
punishment with the quality of education? Nothing. There's
nothing anyone can give you or do for you that grants him or
her the right to abuse or mistreat you."

When people maintain strong, healthy boundaries, their emotional responses have boundaries, too. Healthy people can distinguish between a reason for someone's bad behavior ("He came from an abusive home") and an excuse for it (there is none). They see controlling behavior as abuse and love as love. They do not link them together in their mind, as Helen and Bruce did. By not doing so, they give themselves the permission and the power to respond to the abusive control appropriately, with anger, not free, unconditional forgiveness.

## We Are Often Attracted to Strength

The traditional strength that attracts us to a man often later manifests itself as control. When we begin to understand and accept this idea, the warning signs of abuse (see page 120) become much easier to recognize early on. Many of us grow up believing that men should be strong enough to take care of us no matter how strong we are. Regardless of how smart, accomplished, and secure we are, secretly we often still hope to find a man strong enough to fall back on when things get tough. As we know, men are overconditioned to step into the role of controller, and if we are predisposed to relinquish control over parts of our life, we set the stage for control and abuse. Handing over to your mate any area of responsibility (financial, emotional, psychological) distorts and unequalizes the balance between the two of you.

## We Refuse to Acknowledge How Bad It Really Is

People sometimes protect controllers by refusing to see the bad behavior for what it is and then making excuses for it. When I asked Helen whether Bruce ever emotionally abused her, she replied, "No." But when I asked, "For instance, does he give you the silent treatment or criticize you?" The answer then was "Of course, but that's just the way he is. And when Bruce criticizes me, I know he doesn't really mean it."

When you fail to see criticism for what it is, you step on to a slippery slope. The difference between aggressive criticizing and physical abuse is one of degree only. Even the highest wall of denial cannot block out the knowledge that once we admit to ourselves how bad things are, we will feel uncomfortable until we do something about it.

When we hold ourselves accountable for our own happiness, we seek solutions within ourselves. When we do not, we begin blaming our mate or our circumstances. Granted, it is easier to blame someone or something else than to admit our own mistakes and shortcomings. Blaming others absolves us of any obligation to take action. But it also gives our mate control of the relationship. Often when we think we can't take control, the truth is that we won't.

## We Assume We Are at Fault

Ironically, women who do not take responsibility for their own lives often blame themselves for whatever abuse their mate inflicts. This goes beyond just making excuses for him. For example, one day, Bruce discovered that the checking account was short two hundred dollars. As he angrily waved the checking statement in her face, Helen mentally reviewed every check she had written that month. It took her less than a minute to conclude that the missing money was probably a check she had written to their church. Without even looking at the statement, the checkbook, or the canceled checks, Helen assumed that she was responsible for the missing funds. She didn't ask Bruce whether perhaps he or the bank had made some mistake (which was the case); that possibility never crossed her mind. And when Bruce went into a rage because of the money, neither he nor she assumed he was at fault for not controlling his emotions. Helen automatically assumed she was the guilty party and accepted Bruce's abusive behavior.

Martyrs often ask themselves, *What did I do wrong to deserve this? What is wrong with me? What can I do to regain his love and approval?* Martyrs assume any mistake is their fault, and they readily accept full blame just because their mate has heaped it on them. Martyrs and dependents instinctively question themselves first when criticized—*Is that how I am or what I did?* In contrast, controllers automatically defend themselves first when attacked and ponder these possibilities later, if ever. People who habitually think that they are at fault beat themselves up, which gives their mate an enormous advantage. His right to control her goes unchallenged while her self-esteem withers and her boundaries fade, paving the way for greater, more serious abuse.

Blaming yourself not only lets him off the hook, but it also makes it impossible for you to become angry and assertive enough to demand a change. In the classic pattern, the woman will be justifiably furious over something, then begin chanting a mantra of forgiveness that begins "I did things wrong here, too. I'm not perfect either," saying to him the words she wishes he would say to her. The confusion between normal and healthy makes it hard for you to realize that abuse is *never* justified, no matter what sin you have committed.

### We Refuse to See How We Enable Our Mate's Bad Behavior

Nothing but a show of strength can stop abuse. Whether that involves verbally demanding that your mate change or ending the relationship altogether depends on the severity of the control and the abuse. What you do has more effect than anything you might say. Just the fact that you are still with a man after he behaves badly tells him that you will put up with such behavior. Opting to stay rather than leave not only tells him that the abuse can continue, but it also gives him more opportunities to control and abuse you.

I know this is a difficult concept for most women to grasp, but the truth is that unless your mate understands that you might leave him if things do not change, your complaints have no muscle. It may strike you as mean, aggressive, or unladylike to issue ultimatums (see the Four Steps to Healthy Communication, page 80) because you find yourself mired in beliefs that don't work in this situation: "Kill him with kindness," "You can catch more flies with honey than with vinegar," and "Do unto others as you would have them do unto you." Just remember, it's no coincidence that controllers often end up with partners who live by these precepts.

### We Indulge in Whining and Forgiving Instead of Fighting

Martyrs believe that they are expressing themselves, fighting back, and recouping the balance in the relationship when they nag, whine, blame, and get revenge. They believe these are the only ways they can ever win. This problem is that when you choose these flimsy weapons, you not only are doomed to lose again, but you also usually end up harming both yourself and the relationship. These behaviors alienate and degrade your mate, destroy the personal boundaries necessary for a healthy relationship, and erode your confidence. And no wonder: They do not work. If anything, they make matters worse.

If we are locked in to this type of passive, begging behavior, it is probably because we believe that anger is bad and forgiving and forgetting is better. Any time Bruce was abusive with Helen, for example, he would go out and return with flowers afterward. Then he would tearfully beg her forgiveness, tell her how good she was and how lucky he was to have her, and swear it would never happen again. Before therapy, Helen would take this as proof that Bruce did love her. She actually spent more time worrying about how upset Bruce was than being angry about how he had treated her. In her haste to put the bad feelings behind her, Helen forgave prematurely—before she had emotionally processed the incident and held him accountable, before he apologized, and before his behavior changed. Eventually, Helen realized that forgiveness should be earned, not expected.

## How Playing the Martyr Ultimately Kills Love

It would seem that the person whose mate permits bad behavior has it made: He takes, and she gives, convinced she is working toward a reward—his love and approval. In fact, however, the points you may earn for tolerating bad behavior can be cashed in only for more bad behavior. You may call it love, and it may even look and feel like love, but it's really just more abuse. It seems illogical, but if you look at it from the controlling partner's point of view, it makes perfect sense.

> Ron and Terri entered counseling in the hopes of saving their twenty-four-year marriage. They had been together since high school, raised two great children, and now found themselves disillusioned with their relationship. They had recently separated because, according to Terri, Ron felt nothing for her but disrespect and disgust. Throughout their relationship, she had put him on a pedestal, let him have his way in everything, and played the part of dutiful wife and mother. Even though she alternated between admiring Ron and thinking him a jerk, Terri still felt that at this stage of life she should be rewarded with Ron's attention and love. Instead, she was facing the possible end of a marriage that had evolved into more of a parent-child relationship than a partnership of equals. By never standing up to him, by readily agreeing with him, and by putting up with his criticism and his explosive behavior, she had allowed Ron to be abusive. Now he was ready to leave her. Why?
>
> Ron admitted that he could be short-tempered and that he had little respect for Terri, explaining, "She is always monitoring my behavior in a corrective way, telling me how I'm supposed to feel and psychoanalyzing me. I wish she

would stop blaming me for everything and take some responsibility for what goes on in this relationship. She doesn't realize how tough it is, always making the decisions about everything and then catching hell when things don't turn out right. She's constantly upset and disappointed and believes everything is my fault. I could use a little support once in a while, too."

Though Terri was unhappy with the way Ron treated her, she took pride in never telling him directly what she wanted, but then she made him feel guilty when he didn't give it to her. For one typical example, she wanted flowers for her birthday. Of course, she never bothered to tell Ron this, yet later that evening she said, "Joe loved Catherine enough to get something as romantic as flowers for her birthday." After watching Terri pout for a while, Ron started to leave to go get some flowers for her, thinking that would make her happy. But Terri snapped, "If you're going to get me some flowers now, forget it. It's too late. I don't want them." Terri, like many women who play the martyr, believed that this kind of manipulative behavior is morally superior to that of people who come right out and ask for what they want. What women like Terri fail to realize is that by not telling someone what she wants because she believes he should know, she abdicates her power to influence the relationship and ends up feeling—and being—abused.

When I explained to Terri that she shared the blame for their problems, she became upset and threatened to quit therapy because I didn't understand her. "You don't get it. I had no choices. Ron is so intimidating. He tells me that his way is the right way, and if I disagree, he doesn't let up until I either agree with him or pretend that I do. So I just keep quiet and let him think he's right."

When I finally got her to admit that Ron was not always right about everything, I asked why she let him intimidate her. "It's easier than fighting with him," she answered. After I had outlined very specific ways to force Ron to stop behaving abusively—such as leaving his presence when he became verbally abusive—Terri adamantly disagreed with me.

"I shouldn't have to do that. He should know that I don't like him treating me that way." Deep down, Terri felt that expressing anger is mean and wrong. Having been hurt by the relentless, abusive anger of her father and then that of Ron, she had decided early on never to use anger herself. As a result, she was defenseless. Because she did not know how to confront others and fight for herself, she gave Ron full responsibility—and fully blamed him—for how she felt. By not clearly demanding that he change, she tacitly complied with and enabled Ron's abuse. Ron would get frustrated by never knowing how to make Terri happy, and lose control.

For Terri, finally realizing how she contributed to Ron's bad behavior really opened her eyes. She began to stand up to Ron, but it was too late. She eventually divorced Ron and took control of her own life. Although her marriage could not be saved, Terri vowed that she would never again place her mate on a pedestal and make the mistakes of expecting him to read her mind, and playing the martyr.

Terri and Ron's experience illustrates a key point: People tend to treat us according to the way we act. If we act like a victim, a martyr, a nag, or a whiner, we will be treated like one. By relinquishing her half of the responsibility and the control, Terri became a child, and Ron treated her like one. To put herself in a position where she could demand that Ron change his behavior, Terri had to change her own behavior first. This required her taking responsibility for her part in the relationship. Martyrs are often reluctant to do this since it brings home the powerful and frightening realization that they alone are responsible for their own lives. Given the choice between bravely rowing a sturdy boat down the middle of an uncharted stream and paddling a leaky boat close to the shore, we tend to opt for the latter. Perhaps that's because we already know where it's going, and we know we have the skills to keep it on its limited—not to mention limiting—course. But even the partner who is controlling and abusive eventually tires of the ride.

While we tend to focus on the partner who is the target of bad behavior, we have to remember that the one who tends to dominate often does not know any other way. From what I see in my practice, such people are no happier than their mate. They are just as confused about, and dissatisfied with, their relationships as their partner, though for different reasons. Each time a man controls or abuses his mate, he feels bad about himself afterward as well as unloved by her. But his skills for breaking out of the pattern are no better than hers. When he relinquishes control and begins to treat her better and with respect, he may feel upset initially. Eventually, however, he feels better about her and himself.

## How to Stop Playing the Martyr

Ending a pattern of playing the martyr requires that you drop the illusions, the excuses, and the fairy tales and really begin to see things as they are—not as you would like them to be. Tell yourself repeatedly that you are in charge of your own life and that no one else has a right or a valid reason to treat you badly. Vow that you will not only stop allowing your mate to treat you badly but also stand up to anyone who tries to control you in any way. Using the Four Steps to Healthy Communication, make your concerns, desires, and plans known.

### *Make Him Accountable for His Criticism of You*

Martyrs often ask others for criticism because they feel inadequate and mistakenly believe that such criticism will help them improve themselves. Unfortunately, however, people who often solicit criticism about themselves depend on how others view them for their self-esteem. The problem with this is that others judge us according to their own values, not according to ours. For example, my client Beth is happy and fulfilled teaching preschool because she believes her job is important. Her mate,

Patrick, thinks she earns too little money working in a decidedly unglamorous field and is "wasting" her talent and her time. Beth's self-esteem is healthy, so Patrick's opinions (and that's all they are) mean nothing to her; she is comfortable with her values and her choices, and she tells him so. In a martyr, however, Patrick's statements would prompt self-doubt and a loss of confidence. The martyr would hear his comments not as opinions about her choices, which people are bound to have, but as the truth, a judgment of who she is.

No matter how deeply in love you are, neither you nor your mate has the right to judge the other's personal choices and decisions. For example, after Helen had been in therapy a few months, Bruce called her a "bad wife" and a "dummy" when it came to finances. Instead of believing him, she asked him to describe exactly how her behavior was affecting him personally. In doing this, she was forcing him to admit ownership of his feelings rather than just spewing out judgments based on his own values.

### Admit Your Part, and Ask Him to Admit His

If your mate has more control over your relationship than you do or if you remain in a situation in which you are being abused in any way, you are also to blame, no matter what your excuse. I know this is hard for some people to hear, but don't be ashamed. We all allow abuse at times. Unless you can admit that you are responsible for your role, you cannot assume the responsibility that is needed to change.

### Recognize the Early Signs of Abuse, and Stop It

Martyrdom comes from allowing abuse, and abuse is anything that feels hurtful to you. This may include criticizing, ignoring, talking down to, or embarrassing you. The first time someone does anything that makes you feel uncomfortable, stop him. Remember that your partner will discern your boundaries by your reaction or lack of response. If you overlook incidents of abusive behavior—especially those you consider minor—you will give him the green light to dish out more abuse and possibly increase its intensity. Minor abusive behaviors should never be ignored because they almost always lead to further abuse.

Criticism is usually the first stage of abuse. Many people assume we should be able to handle criticism and that being unable to do so is a sign of weakness. That's not true, however. In fact, it's just the opposite. It takes strength to stand up, to let someone know you will accept how he *feels* about your behavior but not his judgment of it. Criticism is only appropriate when we ask someone directly for it, when it is constructive, and when it is offered to achieve some goal (to improve your schoolwork or your job performance).

In some relationships, couples develop sensitive ways of offering and responding to constructive criticism. I know one woman who believes that when it comes to her professional wardrobe, there is no better arbiter of taste than her husband. Although she does not solicit his input every time she gets dressed up, she does welcome his comments. And I know of another couple in which the husband, Mark, asked his wife, Jenny, to let him know when he's talking too much about his work when they are out socially. These are loving, valid forms of criticism. They have been tacitly or directly requested; they are neutral insomuch as they concern an object or a behavior (as opposed to a personality trait), and they are offered in the spirit of helping the mate, not putting him or her down. In these situations, the mate will say, "That's a beautiful shade of green, but it doesn't do as much for your eyes or your hair color as the blue sweater," not "That's ugly" or "You look awful!" Or the mate will say, "I know you put a lot of effort into this recipe. I'm just wondering whether it would taste a little less salty if you cut down on

## Behaviors You May Not Recognize as Abusive

- aggressively judging and criticizing you, your friends, your family, your co-workers, or anyone or anything important to you
- blaming you without ever acknowledging or owning a part in the situation
- insisting that you always do things his way: going where he wants to go, doing what he wants to do, being only with people he likes
- ordering you to do things rather than politely asking if you'll do them
- demanding that you account for every moment you spend away from him
- discussing you behind your back with your friends and family members
- frequently addressing you in a humiliating, condescending, sarcastic, or demeaning manner
- acting jealous and possessive
- isolating you from your friends and family
- yelling, calling you names, and/or damaging property (throwing things around the house, breaking dishes, and so on)

the anchovies next time," not "This is gross! Where did you learn to cook?"

When criticism focuses on who we are as people—not what we did, said, wore, cooked, cleaned, and so on—it crosses the line and becomes suspect. Criticism that is about who you are and is expressed in a judgmental, sarcastic, angry, or condescending tone is never acceptable under any circumstances. Contrary to what those who use this form of control believe, it is never for your own good, it is never offered because he loves you, and it is never warranted. When your mate criticizes you aggressively, unfairly, and judgmentally, he is exercising a form of control.

When he doesn't like something you have said or done, he should express his feelings, not his judgment of you. So a mate might say, "I feel you don't care about me or the kids when you let the housework go," not "You're such a disgusting slob!" Or he might say, "I feel you aren't as interested in sex as you used to be, and it scares me. Is there something you want to talk about?" not "You frigid old bag! What's your problem?" The differences between these two modes of communication are very clear, and so are their purpose and their intent.

### Learn to Spot His Insecurity

Insecure people often seek control over others. Because we all feel insecure at times, we often sympathize with someone who expresses his insecurity, especially if he seems weak, passive, or frightened. When we encounter someone who is aggressive and controlling, we don't always recognize him as being insecure because he does not fit the profile; he isn't what we expect.

In fact, a controlling mate tries to intimidate others because he is weak, not because he is strong. He uses criticism as a distancing technique, subconsciously reasoning that the further he keeps you away, the fewer flaws in him you'll see. Does it work? Yes, because in rejecting you he pushes your acceptance buttons, driving you to chase after his approval even more vigorously. Obviously, this is not good for you, but it works very well for him, since he can maintain his walls while you're busy pulling your own defenses down.

If you see his attempts to criticize, intimidate, and bully you for what they really are, however, setting boundaries and standing up for yourself will be much easier to do. Remember, every time you choose not to call him on his unacceptable behavior, you give him permission to repeat it. If you allow him to criticize you and you do not tell him his behavior is out of line, you not only invite him to continue criticizing you, but you also validate his belief that you are lazy, stupid, inconsiderate, whatever. Remind yourself of your strengths and his weaknesses, and take him down off that pedestal.

Odd as it may sound, someone well practiced in control and intimidation may actually respond to, even respect and trust, a mate who stands up to him. Any time you confront someone, especially early on in a relationship, you risk his choosing to abandon you rather than working things out. If that does happen, at least you will walk away with your self-esteem intact. If he does choose to work on his unhealthy behavior, don't be surprised if the tables turn and he begins seeking your love and approval.

### Be the Strong Woman You Can Be

There have been times in your life when you were strong. Maybe you had to protect yourself or someone else; maybe you stood up to your boss in behalf of a co-worker, or you stood up to an ex who tried to control you. We all have been in situations where we rose to the occasion, maybe even surprising ourselves. Think back to that time and how you felt then, and realize that you can be that strong again any time you choose.

I wrote in Chapter 4, "Expecting Your Mate to Read Your Mind," about issuing ultimatums. But since most of us are averse to issuing them, my words bear repeating. There is nothing wrong with expressing anger or letting your mate know what consequences he risks if he does not change his behavior. If anything, it may be just the little push he needs. On the downside, yes, it is possible that simply by receiving an ultimatum, he will feel justified in ending the relationship. If so, you are free to move on knowing that this relationship would never have become the fulfilling, equal partnership you seek.

Issuing an ultimatum is a serious matter. Always follow these guidelines: Never threaten to do anything you are unable or unwilling to follow through on, and be prepared to follow through on anything you threaten. It would not be wise or ef-

## Signs That Your Mate Really Is Insecure

- He has few friends.
- He acts tough most of the time and may respond in an excessively aggressive manner with anyone who upsets him or tries to get past his wall.
- He is rigid and often talks about what you and other people should and should not do.
- He is unable to be spontaneous; the slightest change in plans bothers him.
- He still seeks his parents' approval in all aspects of his life; he believes that family comes first no matter what and defends his family members whether they are right or wrong.
- He is unable to share his feelings; he often tells you that nothing's wrong but then broods for days.
- He is secretive about his past, his finances, his friends, his family, his work.
- He tries to control you and others so he will not be controlled; other people in his life have learned to give him wide berth and excuse his bad behavior.
- His relationship history is strewn with women who "didn't understand" him, were "always wrong," and "never really loved" him, although he "did everything" for them.

fective to shout twenty times in a month, "The next time you talk to me like that, I'm leaving you," and then never leave. Remember that the power of the ultimatum is not in issuing it (though that can be a heady, powerful moment) but in you both knowing that you can and will follow through on it.

### Confront Your Mate, and Set Boundaries

Learn to set and protect your boundaries as a general rule, especially with your mate. Whenever your mate behaves toward you in a clearly unacceptable manner, bring it to his attention. Use the Four Steps to Healthy Communication to let him know when he is treating you in ways that you do not accept.

To keep your boundary setting from becoming another exercise in blaming your mate for the facets of your life you refuse to control, ask yourself:

- Am I getting some sense of control, power, or release out of always being angry with him? If so, why? Where is this feeling coming from, and what can I do about it?
- Am I clearly and firmly letting my mate know I will not accept his bad behavior? Or am I avoiding the real issue, saying things I don't really mean, or saying nothing at all?
- Have I communicated to him in such a way—by being firm, by giving him fair warning—that he truly believes, and is threatened by the prospect, that I might leave?
- What action can I take immediately that will make clear to him that I will not accept the way he is treating me?

Once you are sure that you've kept your house in order, let him know how you feel, and describe precisely what consequences he can expect the next time he violates the boundary.

### Resolve Issues from the Past to Strengthen Yourself for Today

If you have suffered an injustice in the past that you believe is still haunting you, confront the person who hurt you, if that's possible. If you discover that your mate makes you feel exactly the same way one of your parents did, work on issues with that parent. Working on these problems at the source often dilutes your mate's power to tap into them. Perhaps your father controlled your mother, and she accepted it, or vice versa. Maybe in your social group, controlling, even mildly abusive, behavior is considered normal. If possible, talk to your father and mother. Ask them why they behaved as they did; then tell them how their behavior affected you. Resolve, and let everyone know, that you will not behave like a martyr anymore and that any relationships you have must change to reflect that, or they must end.

## Take More Responsibility for, and Control of, Your Own Life—Not His

Get your life in order. It is very difficult to project strength and confidence when you confront your mate if you are afraid that breaking up will leave you broke, lonely, jobless, and/or friendless. Any area of your life that you do not control—be it physical, financial, emotional, or social—is an area in which you are vulnerable to your mate's control and to others. Be honest in assessing your strengths and weaknesses. If you need to secure your financial future, you may want to get a job and/or consult an attorney about how best to protect yourself within the marriage. If you feel you need emotional support, reach out to friends and other loved ones. If your entire social life revolves around his family, his friends, and his co-workers, start building your own support network.

Make time to be alone, to think about how your life may be better without him. Even if you can fairly and honestly attribute a relationship's decline to other factors, ultimately most women will walk out secretly wondering whether they have failed personally. Now is the time to remind yourself of your strong points. In one of my most insecure moments, as a relationship was ending, I told myself, *You're attractive, intelligent, and together* (the three things I least believed at that moment). I repeated that sentence to myself one hundred times, and by the eighty-seventh repetition, I actually began to believe it. Feeling stronger, I went out and met someone new who treated me wonderfully.

# A Last Word on Playing the Martyr

Martyrdom is not only destructive and self-defeating, but it is also extremely unattractive. You may feel insecure, and your mate may make you feel even more so, but in truth controllers are often more insecure than you imagine—even more insecure than you. The big difference between you and him is that he hides it better behind a wall of criticism, control, and abuse. Stop accepting his judgmental version of who you are. No matter what he or anyone else believes, you are lovable. No one you have ever known and no one you will ever meet ever has the right to treat you badly. When he criticizes you to make you feel bad, don't wait for him to make you feel better. Grab the reins and do it yourself. The best way to start is to stand up to him, set boundaries, follow through with consequences if he crosses them, seek out people who treat you well, and never look back.

# 6

# Mistake Number Four:
# Thinking You Are Always Right

Not long after Alan and I began dating, we were cooking one of our first meals together. He was preparing the mashed potatoes, and when I noticed him slicing the raw potatoes instead of cutting them into chunks, I blurted out, "That's not how you're supposed to cut potatoes!" Startled by the realization that I sounded exactly like my mother, I caught myself. "I'm sorry," I said. "I can't believe I said that. It doesn't matter how you cut the potatoes. What am I thinking?" Why was I, of all people, trying to tell Alan how to cook? I'm not even a good cook, and I can't stand it when other people behave as if they had all the answers. And, besides, who really cares how he cuts the potatoes?

I'm sharing this story because it illustrates some of the difficulties in recognizing and correcting self-righteous behavior. For many of us, behaving self-righteously comes so naturally that we often don't even realize we're doing it. Unfortunately, many of those toward whom we take a self-righteous attitude—

especially mates—believe this is normal behavior in someone they love. That does not mean they like it; they probably don't. Yet once again, we find ourselves at the mercy of antiquated, false beliefs about human nature and love. We believe that loving someone gives us the right to criticize and correct him, and when he does not behave or think as we believe he should, we believe we can punish him as well. Why? Well, because we're right. Right? Wrong.

People who act as if they were always right put themselves in the controlling role and damage their relationship by demeaning, insulting, and punishing their mate. Sometimes that is their intention, but usually those who think they are always right have more subtle, complex issues at work and are blind to the effects of their behavior. The behaviors that emerge from this attitude range from such seemingly minor offenses as interrupting and nagging to chronic psychological and even physical abuse. These behaviors throw the relationship off balance and inevitably kill love because whenever words or actions send the message "I'm right," the sometimes silent postscript reads, "and you're wrong."

### A Dozen Communication Don'ts

1. Don't criticize.
2. Don't advise.
3. Don't interrogate.
4. Don't isolate.
5. Don't nag.
6. Don't threaten.
7. Don't blame.
8. Don't physically intimidate.
9. Don't pressure.
10. Don't harass.
11. Don't judge.
12. Don't manipulate.

## What's Wrong with Believing You're Right

You are probably saying to yourself, *But I usually do have the right answers. That's not the same thing.* And you are correct. You may know a great deal about things and reach the best conclusion more often than not. You and your mate may have agreed to defer to one or the other of you in specific areas of expertise: He may be better at cooking; you may excel at financial matters. You may even seek the other's help and advice in these areas, and it may be given freely and in the interest of helping.

What I am referring to here, however, is a persistent, chronic, almost automatic assumption that you alone possess the only possible right answer to every problem in life, from how to cut potatoes to how your mate should behave toward you. You may have a problem with believing you are always right if you

- criticize, degrade, and/or humiliate your mate—"You're just too stupid to get it!"
- judge your mate and try to dictate to him as if he were your child—"You should call your mother." "You shouldn't act like that." "You should want to be with me."
- speak condescendingly by advising, lecturing, and/or directing—"You really should quit your job." "It would be better if your mother didn't visit so often; she just brings you down."
- let your mate know you do not respect or are not interested in what he has to say by interrupting, changing the subject, or ignoring him.
- rarely, if ever, admit your mistakes or problems or try to minimize what you said—"I didn't really say that, and even if I did, you should know that I didn't mean it."
- make sexist comments that indirectly put your mate down—"Why should it surprise me. You're acting like a typical man, aren't you?"

- try to scare your mate into letting you have your way—
"You better think about what I said before you do that."
- threaten your mate that there will be consequences if he
doesn't follow your advice or do something your way—
"I know you won't be happy going back to school.
When you start having problems, I don't want to hear
about it."
- always remind your mate when he is wrong—"I told
you so."

When we exhibit this behavior, we trample the respect
and tolerance that our mate—and everyone—deserves. No
two people will ever share all the same ideas, opinions, and
feelings no matter how much they love each other. And the
fact that your partner agrees with you does not mean that he
loves you more than he would if he disagreed.

Often when I point this out to clients, they indicate they
know that two people cannot always agree. Yet outside my office, they still expect their mate to see things their way. If our
brains know that it doesn't really matter to us how our mate
cuts the potatoes, votes in the election, or thinks about subjects that do not directly affect our relationship, why do we
still find ourselves pointing these things out, trying to be
right?

Holly and Dan had been in a traditional marriage for ten
years. Dan earned all the family income while Holly stayed
home raising their two children and running the house.
Through most of their marriage, each had been telling the
other what he or she should and shouldn't do. Dan constantly told Holly how she should clean the house, in what
order she should run errands, and how the flower boxes
should be planted. If you asked him, he would say he was
only helping her by pointing out what she was doing
wrong so she could do it right. Typically, they argued,
Holly ended up doing things her way, and then Dan anx-

iously waited for something to go wrong so he could say, "I told you so."

Like many people, Dan really did believe there is one way—and only one way—in which to do things. In one session, he and Holly were arguing about whether the Kitty Litter should be scooped out as the cat used it or dumped out and replaced all at one time. When I said it was a personal preference, Dan began arguing with me: "Everybody *knows* you should scoop scoopable Kitty Litter!" Dan, who likes being right, also had an argument on his side. Since he was the sole breadwinner and since every time Holly dumped the litter, it cost more money than it would have if she'd done it his way, Dan felt justified in pressing his point.

Yes, dumping all the litter does cost more, but the real reason Dan picked on Holly was that he resented and disrespected her for not being what he considers a worthwhile, productive member of society—that is, someone who earns money. Dan often insinuated that the day Holly started bringing home a paycheck, she could have some say in how the money was spent.

Though Dan believed he'd kept his true feelings well disguised, Holly got his message loud and clear. She felt devalued by him, and so she retaliated by competing with him. For instance, when Dan took a new position that required some travel yet tripled their income, he expected Holly to be excited and supportive. Instead, she was jealous of his new perks. When he said he was tired or complained about work, she would snap, "What do you have to complain about? You probably had a two-hour lunch in a fancy restaurant with an attractive female customer or played a round of golf today!" Instead of offering support, she seemed to feel pleasure when anything went wrong for him.

Like her husband, Holly had her own list of unspoken grievances. She had never told Dan that she resented being stuck home chauffeuring the kids while he was out in the exciting world of business. Instead, she had self-righteously begun to hound Dan more than ever, tried to make him feel guilty about enjoying his new job, and accused him of not participating enough in her and the family's activities. She continually told Dan what he should do to be a better husband and father. A typical exchange went like this:

HOLLY: "A good husband should want to hang out around the house on the weekends and help with the chores. You told me you'd sweep the garage."

DAN: "But I make plenty of money, and we can pay someone to sweep the garage, for Christ's sake."

HOLLY: "That's not the point. A good husband and father should act like a part of the family. I want you here participating in the chores no matter how much money you make."

DAN: "Fine. I'll participate. Instead of playing golf today, we'll do something fun, OK?"

HOLLY: "That doesn't solve the problem of the garage. Don't you even want to be a good husband and father and do what you should do?"

DAN: "OK, I'll sweep out the damn garage!"

As long as Dan and Holly went on like this, their conflict continued with neither ever getting what he or she really wanted. In counseling, both Holly and Dan admitted that their shoulds came directly from their parents. Neither ever questioned whether he or she truly believed in the traditional roles they assumed, or thought of doing things differently simply because they wanted to. Tellingly, when I asked them whether they wanted a marriage that was like either of their parents' marriages, both replied no.

Holly and Dan struggled for a long time and almost ended their relationship more than once, but with therapy they managed to save their marriage. For the first time, they began to tell each other how they felt instead of nagging and criticizing. Dan finally told Holly that he felt he was not important in her life. She revealed that she wanted him to be a "team player" at home. He countered by suggesting that she get a job and focus on her own happiness and achievement instead of constantly putting down his. At first, she resisted, but eventually she came around to seeing Dan's point of view and admitted that she wanted a life outside the family, too. She apologized for behaving like a mother to him, and he apologized for acting like her father. Once the real issues were out in the open, it was much easier for them to let go of the petty ones; Dan even decided he didn't really care about how the Kitty Litter was changed.

## Why We Feel We Need to Be Right

### We Try to Overcompensate for Our Insecurities

We all have insecurities, and it's only normal to try to hide them. Acting as if we know more than someone else creates the temporary illusion that we are stronger, smarter, somehow better. For better or worse, sometimes people actually do believe in our front, and so we hit on an effective ego defense, which we use again and again. Unfortunately, while we are distracting others from seeing who we really are, we are also keeping them at a distance. It is impossible for anyone to forge a truly intimate relationship with someone who keeps hiding behind the façade of self-righteousness.

Thinking we are always right is a hard habit to break because parents, teachers, and other authority figures encouraged and rewarded us for perfecting it. Continually measured against our classmates or siblings, we quickly learned to earn favor by showing up the competition. We each possess a range of skills and different kinds of intelligence, but these often remain underdeveloped and underappreciated at the expense of our learning to be intellectually or morally right. The rewards for equally important qualities—such as tolerance, maturity, sound judgment, flexibility, and fairness—are not as obvious or as readily available as those for being right—the gold star, the promotion, winning the fight.

## *It Seems Like the Right Thing to Do*

If you think back to the arguments you witnessed at home, you probably cannot recall very many that ended in a truce or were resolved with an agreement to disagree. Chances are no dispute could end until someone was proclaimed right and someone else was proclaimed wrong. Because we often bring to our relationships behaviors we model after those of our parents, it is easy to fall into the pattern of viewing any disagreement with our mate in terms of right and wrong.

When we pick on the little things our mate does—how he squeezes the toothpaste tube from the middle, puts half-empty ice-cube trays back in the freezer, and buys the wrong brand of margarine—it may be because we observed a parent, usually our mother, asserting authority over her or his only sphere of influence—in our mother's case, the home and the kids. For many women of our parents' generation, child rearing and housekeeping were the only arenas in which they were allowed to make the rules. A host of experts bullied moms into adopting the absolutely correct, scientifically proven way of doing everything around the house, from scrubbing the floors to ensuring Junior's intellectual development. It was all Mom's responsibility, and any failure—from ring around the collar to Suzy's dropping out of college—was hers to bear. No wonder mothers often seemed persistently, even irrationally concerned about the right way to do things and were so quick to argue with, nag at, punish, or browbeat objectors. Mother may have extended this attitude to include Dad as well. Within that unequal, traditional relationship, Mom's unchallenged reign over house and hearth may have served some purpose, perhaps even giving the two of them the illusion that the relationship was more balanced than it was.

Again, we have an example of normal but unhealthy behavior that we subconsciously carry into our own relationships. This is how Mom dealt with Dad, so this is how we deal with our mate, and we rarely question it. Men often go along because they, too, learned from watching their parents. They took the same lessons; they adopted the male husband-father role in much the same way we fell into the wife-mother role. We're both doing what we think we're supposed to do. Just remember, you cannot behave like a parent toward your mate without treating him like a child, and this is a surefire way to kill love and passion.

Just because your mate shrugs and claims he doesn't care which picture hangs where, what color scheme you choose, or what you have for dinner that night, if you habitually make a point of getting your way, he will resent you. If you find yourself constantly feeling you must win on minor matters like these, chances are that like Dan and Holly you are continually vying for more control of the relationship.

## *We Believe There Is Only One True Right and Wrong*

Many people do believe that the concepts of right and wrong are absolute and beyond discussion. This is particularly true when it comes to religion and politics, where some people define themselves by their beliefs. With so many points of view on any subject, it would seem impossible for any way to be the only right one. Yet for some people, there really is only one right way, and everyone who disagrees is wrong and evil. This is the "logic" that breeds racism, sexism, and homophobia. To such people, being right bestows on them the moral authority, even an obligation, to criticize, abuse, and punish those whom they deem wrong.

Generally, people who hold such extreme views end up with a mate who shares them. Sometimes people who grow up with very strict or extreme views reject them but carry over a black-and-white way of looking at everything else. In other words, they may not choose the same "right" way their parents chose, but whichever way they do pick will be the only right way. For example, Ted, a thirty-year-old accountant, was turned off by his mother's Christian fundamentalism, so he forbade any and all religious beliefs in his house.

In real life, moral absolutes are few and far between. Even in a list of *shoulds* as widely accepted as the Ten Commandments, reasonable people can allow for exceptions. For example, if you are being attacked, it's generally considered appropriate to kill to save your life. Everything from honoring your parents to lying has circumstances under which it is appropriate to break the rule. In their attempt to teach us right from wrong, our parents bombarded us with shoulds and shouldn'ts. Consequently, the more complex gray areas, the exceptions, and the acceptable alternatives were rarely addressed, and few of us ever learned how to compromise.

It is important to remember that people who cling tenaciously to extreme, narrow definitions of right and wrong are fighting for more than their position. More often than not, they feel that their very self-identity is on the line as well, and this need to protect their identity isn't limited only to the big issues. We think in terms of right and wrong all the time, even when it comes to subjects we have no emotional investment in. Take two people arguing over the right way to eat spaghetti, whether a bride should wear white, or whether it's wrong for children to address adults by their first name. Granted, one alternative may be more socially acceptable, more in keeping with tradition, or more popular. But that alone does not make it right, nor does it make the person who chooses the other course wrong.

## We Want Control over Others

We grow up believing that control over others gives us more control over our own lives. In fact, however, it rarely does. All it does is give us more responsibility to bear and more reason to resent those over whom we can exert our influence. Power—or the ability to influence, guide, or dictate the terms of a relation-ship—is what every struggle in a relationship ultimately is about. It begins when you meet someone you like and evaluate whether he is "good enough" for you. Eventually, one person's ability to influence and direct the relationship waxes and wanes as the two of you get a better sense of each other's personality, boundaries, and beliefs. It may be appropriate for one of you to take more control sometimes. Or you may both agree that one area is his department and the other is yours. At the end of the day, however, the score should be a wash.

Intimacy requires vulnerability, and as we allow ourselves to be vulnerable, we often feel threatened. We attempt to pro-tect ourselves by asserting more control than is healthy. When two people commit themselves to each other, they may find themselves competing to determine what they, in their newly merged identity as a couple, will say, think, and do.

Michael and Colleen had lived together happily for four years before they married. Both in their mid-twenties, they loved going out, splurging on last-minute romantic get-aways, and just being together. But just two months after their wedding, they were in my office on the verge of sepa-rating. Their arguments went like this:

MICHAEL: "What happened to you? You used to like going out and having fun. Now that we're married, you say we can't get away to Aspen for the weekend until we put four hundred dollars into savings, and we can't rent a houseboat in the Keys next fall because we should be buy-ing china and crystal stemware."

COLLEEN: "Michael, we *are* married, you know. We need to be more serious about these things now."

MICHAEL: "But why? OK, maybe we should save some more money before we go away. But, Colleen, we've been eating off of mismatched Fiestaware now for four years. And, you know what—I don't care! We didn't need china then. Why do we need it now?"

COLLEEN: "Well, I care, and I don't see why I should be the only new bride in town who doesn't have nice new things. Maybe if you started acting like more of a husband, you'd understand what I mean."

MICHAEL: "What do you mean 'act like more of a husband'?"

COLLEEN: "For example, when we go out on weekends, could you try wearing something a little nicer than jeans? What's wrong with Dockers?"

MICHAEL: "Dockers? I may be married, but I'm not retired! Come on, Colleen, there's nothing wrong with my jeans."

COLLEEN: "But, Michael, I don't see any of the other husbands in our neighborhood wearing jeans. It just looks weird to me now. Maybe it's time for you to grow up."

MICHAEL: "Well, if growing up and being married means not having any more fun, then maybe we should just forget it! Colleen, I married you because I love you, and I thought you loved me. I don't understand why you feel like we have to change now just because we're married."

I've counseled many couples who were perfectly happy before they married or moved in together. Then, as if someone flipped a switch somewhere, they began arguing over things they'd never even thought about before. These couples often ask, "If those things didn't bother us before, why are we fighting about them now?"

The answer is that subconsciously we believe "real" couples should think alike and be in agreement on most things and live their lives a certain way. In our mate's agreement and support, we see acceptance and love; in his disagreement or his refusal to go along with us, we sense rejection and worry that he doesn't really love us. The tension arises because even as we move closer together, we instinctively resist our own identity being swallowed up by the larger entity—the partnership, the marriage, the relationship. Suddenly, faulty reasoning kicks in, and we start thinking, *If I win the argument, my identity remains intact. If I lose, however, I relinquish who I am.* Or we assume that if we can force him to admit that he is wrong, we win, but if we admit to an error, we lose. These arguments, then, are often about drawing lines and recalculating the ever-shifting balance between each partner's individuality and the relationship as a whole.

Couples in healthy relationships work this out to their satisfaction by keeping their individual identities, respecting their differences, compromising, negotiating, and sometimes agreeing to disagree. For couples entrenched in this continual play for power, however, who wins and who loses must be determined at any cost. No relationship can survive in this competitive atmosphere for long.

## *We Believe in Punishing Others for Their Bad Behavior*

Since most of us resist attempts to change us, we often view punishment as our only recourse when our mate resists our own attempts to change him. Nagging, complaining, withholding love or attention, and otherwise trying to hurt a mate are all forms of punishment. Odd as it sounds, we punish those we love out of a desire to be closer to them. We confuse their unwillingness to please us by changing who they are with lack of love for us; and we view punishment as a surefire technique to force that change. When a particular punishment fails to yield the desired result, we don't conclude that the punishment itself is a losing game (which it is), only that a more severe punishment is called for.

Sometimes a woman who punishes her mate displays a constant façade of anger, letting her mate know dozens of times a day that she doesn't approve of his behavior, and he then feels he can't do anything right. Others who cannot express their anger appropriately get caught up in what I call the Punishment Cycle. The first phase, the Setup, begins when she (or he) starts to stockpile old hurts and resentments instead of voicing them in a healthy manner. When the pressure becomes too great, she either explodes at or withdraws from her mate, beginning the Punishment Phase. While she may believe in punishment, she knows that she has hurt her mate, so she begins feeling guilty and moves into the Make-Up Phase, temporarily bending over backward to please him and promising she will never do it (the hurtful behavior) again. Of course, nowhere in the cycle has the couple confronted or resolved the problems that led to the Setup, so before long the cycle begins anew. The more someone punishes, the more guilty she feels, and the more she blames and resents her mate for making her feel that way.

Because we recall punishment as an effective tool that our parents and teachers used to change our behavior, we think it will work with our mate. The fatal flaw here is that while we concentrate on how the person who punished us was in control and got what he or she wanted from us, we tend to forget how the punishment made us feel: humiliated, hurt, and less lovable.

Your mate is an adult, not a child. When a caring adult punishes a child, ideally it is to shape him or her into a person who will be moral, well behaved, self-disciplined, and so on. A child is a work in progress whose own inclinations and ideas may be unacceptable or dangerous to himself or herself and others. Your mate, on the other hand, is an adult, a done deal, so to speak. When you tell him what he should and should not do, you are trying to change his personal identity, showing disrespect for him as a person, and trying to assert more influence over him than is healthy. Don't fool yourself: If you manage to persuade your mate to change through punishment, he will resent you. The only healthy way to get your mate to change the way he treats you is by setting boundaries with him (which was discussed in Chapter 5, "Playing the Martyr," and other chapters).

## Do the Right Thing: Learn to Be a Partner, Not a Parent

### *Admit That You Don't Have All the Answers*

If you have been acting as if you were always right, chances are you've been doing it longer and more often than you realize. This is a pattern you will need patience and help from your mate to break. First, don't deny that you do it. Admit to yourself that you have an attitude problem, and face the fact that it is damaging your relationship. For many of us, self-righteous behavior becomes a habit, and the best way to break bad habits is to replace them with good habits.

### *Identify Opposing Values*

As children, we accepted our parents' values, but as teenagers we were swayed by the values of peers, values that were sometimes in opposition to those of our parents. By the time we settled into a serious relationship, we found ourselves coming full circle and embracing some of our parents' values again. This is often a point of confusion for us personally and a source of contention between us and our mate. Many of our ideas about what is right and wrong within the context of a committed relationship, a shared household, and a family derive from what we learned in our childhood home. When we and our mate come into conflict on these issues, it is often because each of us is defending "inherited" beliefs and values that we never questioned before. Most of us don't know how to respond, so we react defensively.

During a therapy session, Michael asked Colleen why whenever they had company over, everything had to be different. He ran down a list of things Colleen insisted on because they were "proper": using linen rather than paper napkins, serving salad as the last course instead of the first, offering cream instead of skim milk with coffee. Colleen responded that this was "how people do things," but when pressed to explain why she chose to, she didn't really know beyond the fact that this was how her mother entertained.

We begin to change by evaluating what we say we believe and asking ourselves why we think as we do. Are these ideas we have always lived with and always assumed were correct? Are these issues we have considered carefully? As I've said, many of the prevailing old values and false beliefs simply do not work today. It's fine to admire your father for being able to totally support his family, but is it realistic in today's economy to expect your mate to do the same? Is it fair to consider him any less of a man because he, like millions of other men today, cannot? Or he may measure you against his mother, who stayed at home, kept an immaculate house, and always served a five-course dinner. Are you really less of a wife or mother because your kids consider pizza one of the basic food groups?

We must examine our beliefs carefully, especially those that pertain to how people should behave as lovers, mates, and spouses. We need to think of our values in terms of what they mean to us today, and we must ask our mate to do the same. You may even consider drawing up a relationship contract and revising it at different points in your lives. In it, you should spell out your individual and shared expectations, decisions, and plans. Of course, people, circumstances, and goals do change, but nothing here is written in stone. The purpose of this exercise is to force you and your mate to think about, discuss, and establish where you each stand on particular issues.

One couple I saw agreed that once they had children, he would try to avoid being transferred more than once every seven or eight years, or he would look for another job. Michael and Colleen agreed to split their savings between a long-term account and one used solely for entertainment and travel.

### Admit Your Mistake to Him

Step out of the controlling role in your relationship. Get into the habit of admitting that you were wrong each time you act self-righteously or punitively. Admit that you shouldn't have treated your mate the way you did, and offer to make it up to him. Be sincere and vulnerable. Accept responsibility for your behavior, and apologize. Resist the temptation to swear you'll never do it again or beat yourself up over it; this will only make you more likely to slip up again.

Empower your mate to help you stop. Work out a signal your mate can give you when you lapse into self-righteous behavior. You may be surprised how many times a day you behave this way without even knowing it. I enlisted a female friend to help me break my self-righteous habit. We were together and had just gotten out of the car when she began walking one way and I instinctively said, "No, let's go this way."

"Aye, aye, Captain," she replied, and I got the message. I apologized immediately and resolved to improve my behavior next time. You and your mate might agree that he will say, "Honey, you're doing it again," "Yes, ma'am," or "The way you said that hurts me," for example.

### Monitor Your Bad Behavior

Stop the behavior. Stop acting as if you are always right. Whenever you sense a condescending comment, an unsolicited bit of advice, or a defensive reaction hopping up and down on the tip of your tongue, ask yourself, *Is this really important? Does it really matter to me if it's done his way instead of mine?* If it does matter, then count to ten, monitor your tone of voice and your choice of words, then begin with a statement of feeling (not thinking), and offer a reason why you feel as you do. Instead of "you know you shouldn't wear jeans to that cocktail party," try "I have to admit that it will upset me if you wear jeans because it is important to me how these people view me. Please dress up for me, honey."

Prepare yourself by setting up specific situations and planning how you would like to respond. Each time you find yourself apologizing to your mate for acting as if you were right, be sure to tell him how you hope to handle the situation the next time. For example, "I'm sorry that I took out my anger at my business partner on you tonight. The next time I feel myself beginning to lash out at you instead of her, I will excuse myself, go into the bedroom, and punch some pillows until I calm down." A friend of mine told her mate, "I know it hurts you when I call you names, and I apologize. From now on, whenever I call you a name, I will pay you a dollar. If I cannot get this under control by the time we reach one hundred, I promise I will go into therapy." Or you could say, "I'm disappointed in the way I behaved last night. It was wrong of me to interrupt you constantly while you were speaking to our guests. The next time I feel compelled to do that, I will excuse myself for a few minutes until I can get myself under control."

### Express Feelings Instead of Opinions

It is very hard to argue with someone's feelings. If you say, "What you just said really hurt my feelings," you will be far less likely to pick a fight than if you say, "That's wrong," "You shouldn't have said that," or "Only a really mean person would say something like that." Strive to be human, not perfect, and that means being vulnerable at times. You can often take the heat out of an argument simply by saying what you feel rather than what you think: "I'm so upset only because I love you and feel hurt by what you did."

### Discover Why You Feel the Need to Be Right

Ask yourself, *Why am I acting like this? What am I afraid of? Am I trying to convince myself that I'm smart? Why would I treat someone the way I've been treating my mate? Do I feel more in control when I'm telling my mate he's wrong? Is it a role I've played most of my life because I've modeled it after my dad (or mom)? Did it really work for him (or her)? Is it time to give it up?*

It is very common to find that you have a deep-seated fear of not being good enough in some way and that this is the underlying cause of your need to be right. Someone in your childhood or an ex-lover may have criticized you regularly or made you feel inadequate. Face that pain, and then do whatever you must to come to terms with it so you can allow yourself to be more vulnerable and let your mate into your life. This may include therapy, confronting parents and ex-lovers, or making serious changes in your life. Remember that we often try to control the little things in life because the real problem seems invincible. Eliminate the big problem, and the little ones often disappear.

Instead of getting into battles in which no one wins and you and your mate beat at each other over the same issue again and again, agree to disagree. See how powerful it can be to lose one small battle but win the war.

### Learn to Respect Your Differences, and Compromise Creatively

When resolving issues in healthy relationships, both mates show respect for the other's personal values. This does not mean that they agree with them, however, and this is a distinction people sometimes fail to grasp. It means that we know what we and our mate agree on and what we do not agree on. In addition, it means we have a good sense of each issue's relative importance to our mate and, most important, why he feels as he does. Period. When we understand why our mate believes as he does, we feel less threatened and less compelled to try to change his mind.

> Meredith and Kenny come from two totally different backgrounds. Meredith's parents are fairly well off, whereas Kenny's are poor. Although both are now successful plastic surgeons, Kenny was, in his wife's words, "cheap." For his part, Kenny felt Meredith was wastefully extravagant, especially when it came to gifts. During one therapy session, Kenny cried as he described the impoverished holidays of his childhood. For the first time, Meredith understood the pain motivating his behavior, something she admitted she had never truly understood before. She also realized there was room in their marriage for both their opinions and that how much he chose to spend on gifts really had nothing to do with her. They also reached a compromise on joint gifts: He promised to contribute a little more, and she promised to spend a little less.

While it is important for couples to learn to compromise when they can, it is equally important for them to identify those points on which compromise is out of the question. For example, you may be a fierce Democrat, and he may be a dedicated Republican. You can simply agree to disagree. Some points almost demand complete agreement (the decision of whether or not to have children, for example), some require a high level of agreement with some room for compromise (where you will live), and others are either easily negotiated (how the holidays will be spent) or simply not worth fighting about (what we're having for dinner). Don't sweat the small stuff. Before you respond to your mate, ask yourself, *Does this really matter to me? If so, why? If not, why don't I just let it go?*

My friend Maria is a Christian, and her husband, Seth, is Jewish. While he respects his religion's heritage, as he does that of all religions, he also loves Christmas. They decorate a tree, and their son believes in Santa Claus, but they agree not to display religious symbols, like nativity scenes and crosses. Maria was surprised, therefore, when Seth objected to her placing a decorated wreath on the front door. When she asked him why, he replied, "It makes me uncomfortable because where I grew up, only the very conservative Christians decorated outside at Christmas. I know this seems illogical, but since we don't let either faith dominate our lives, I don't think we should at Christmastime either." Although his seemingly contradictory behavior baffled most of Maria's family, she thought it over and concluded that Seth's feelings came first. Their compromise: hanging the wreath from the staircase banister or from the mantel.

On the issues on which compromise is not possible, when you totally disagree with your mate, get into the habit of listening respectfully, accepting his point of view, and saying so. You might say, for example, "I understand how you could see it that way," or "Now that you've explained why you feel that way, it makes sense to me." Be sure your mate understands that you do respect his opinion before stating your own: ". . . but I'd also like you to see my point. Will you listen while I explain how I see it?" This way you have shown respect and asked for respect in return.

Although we are rarely taught them, there are effective ways to state your differences without prompting a defensive reaction. For example, "*I believe* it's a good idea for couples to spend their weekends alone together because I feel that it helps them catch up after a hectic week. *You think* that we should each be able to see our friends on weekends because you think couples benefit by having outside interests and strong friendships. So let's compromise and spend one day together and one day with our individual friends."

Remind yourself and your mate that there are many paths to resolving each issue; complete agreement is not the only or even the best way to go. Keep in mind that you do not necessarily need to have an opinion about everything (do you *really* care whether the butter is kept in a covered dish or on an uncovered plate?) and that some problems simply do not have easy solutions (your husband, who is an only child, must oversee the care of his father, who suffers from Alzheimer's disease). Give yourself the opportunity to see that your differences as people can be your strength as a couple. Alan and I have accepted that we have very different levels of patience. When a situation calls for Alan's calm, easy persistence, I say, "You handle this one." When we need something to be handled quickly, he turns it over to me.

### Control Yourself, Not Him

Stop thinking of punishment as a means to an end, and recognize it for what it is: a symptom of your failure to communicate what you really want effectively. You can stop the Punishment Cycle at any point simply by communicating honestly and openly. In fact, simply by following the Four Steps to Healthy Communication, you almost guarantee that the initial Setup Phase never begins.

If you find yourself starting the cycle again, take these steps:

### How to Stop the Punishment Cycle

- Stop the Setup Phase by expressing yourself using the Four Steps to Healthy Communication. For example, "I feel frustrated that I've done the shopping and the cooking for your business dinner and you don't seem to appreciate it. I want you to show me your appreciation by promising you will help me clean up after everyone has left and let me sleep in tomorrow. Will you promise to do that? If not, I won't be able to go with you to your business brunch on Sunday."

- If you have already moved into the Punishment Phase, stop yourself, become vulnerable, and say, "I'm sorry I'm acting like this. I don't mean to hurt you. It's just that I feel you didn't appreciate everything I did for your business dinner. I'm sorry I didn't say something sooner, before I let it get to this. But I need you to promise that next time you will be more considerate and help me clean up." Then let it go.

- If you have already punished your mate and are now in the Make-Up Phase, you have a different task ahead of you. Again, show vulnerability and apologize, but resist the temptation to throw yourself at his mercy because you feel guilty. You might say, "I'm sorry I said and did those things. I know I hurt you, and that behavior was uncalled for. I was angry, however, because I felt you didn't appreciate all I'd done for your dinner party. Even though I spoke in anger and insulted you and shouldn't have, I did mean what I said about wanting you to reciprocate more here at home. I have been feeling unappreciated for a while now. Still, I'm sorry for how I behaved. My behavior this time was not acceptable, and I promise that next time I'll try to be more forthcoming and not let my emotions get out of control like this."

## Build the Intimacy That Makes Compromise Possible

In an intimate, balanced relationship in which a couple compromises and works at finding solutions, no one ever loses. When each partner is secure in knowing that he or she will be the beneficiary of a future compromise, it is easier to give in today without feeling used or cheated. Take some risks; for example, try giving in completely a few times. See your self-righteous behavior for what it really is: a hindrance to intimacy and love.

# 7

## Mistake Number Five:
## Rescuing Your Mate

- Would your mate be lost without you?
- In most ways, are you stronger than he is?
- Has your mate had a harder time in life than most other people?
- Does he have trouble standing on his own without help from family, friends, or you?
- Does he seem to be perpetually unhappy unless you're doing something for him?
- Does he have excuse after excuse as to why he never solves his problems, and/or do you even make excuses for him?

When a woman is asked to list the qualities she looks for in a mate, she invariably includes his ability to be there for her. We often mistakenly think that our being there for someone will cause him to be there for us. In a healthy relationship, each partner assumes responsibility for his or her own life. Each partner loves and wants and cares for the other.

Life can be tough, and one reason we build relationships is partially selfish: to know there will be someone to lean on when things go bad. The ability to open up and allow someone to help us when we truly need help balanced by the willingness to put someone else's needs before our own at times and support that person signifies maturity and strength. Couples who strike and maintain this balance usually enjoy rewarding long-term relationships, for the partners are secure in the knowledge that each can depend on the other to come through in a crisis. In contrast, when one partner allows the other to be in perpetual need and then provides constant support, she is making the mistake of rescuing her mate.

One difference between a healthy relationship and a rescuing one is the way in which the couple defines *crisis*— whether it's something *truly* beyond his control or whether it is a manifestation of his inability to handle his own life. Is his unemployment due to sudden downsizing or to his unwillingness to keep a job? Is his latest financial setback due to a serious health problem or to his compulsive gambling? And when he comes to you in some crisis, what do you two define as *help*? Is it supporting him as he solves his own problems? Or does it mean simply solving his problems for him by giving him the money or carrying the load without asking for anything in return? When we truly help someone, our joint efforts lead to a solution, or at least to a step along the way. Doing everything ourselves is not helping; it's rescuing.

Loving becomes rescuing when we believe we should— or our mate demands that we—solve his problems or protect him from the consequences of his own behavior. We may do too much for him (see Chapter 5, "Playing the Martyr") or think we know what's best for him (see Chapter 6, "Thinking You Are Always Right"). Both these mistakes have much in common with this one, but with some important differences. Whereas a martyr is a dependent, a rescuer is a controller. And whereas someone who thinks she's always right lacks empathy for those she tries to help, a rescuer overempathizes with those she tries to help.

You know you have crossed the line into rescuing if you

- *always* handle his problems, even when doing so puts you in jeopardy, no matter how much it hurts you, how little he reciprocates, and how often he repeats this behavior. For example, you always pay your mate's gambling debts even though you have to work two jobs and forgo your own financial security while he remains unemployed.
- *always* believe and act on what you think is best for your mate no matter how many times your decisions and actions fail to bring about a change in his behavior. For example, you always protect your mate from the consequences of his drinking (you pay his bills, lie to his boss, let him drive your car because he can't insure his own) instead of insisting he get treatment.
- *always* feel at least a twinge of virtuous self-admiration. Unlike a person who thinks she's always right, you feel a sense of reward for having helped out of the goodness of your heart. And unlike the martyr, your ego gets stroked because you think you have resolved someone else's problem.
- *never* demand anything in return, never let him suffer the consequences of his own behavior, never consider any response *but* rescuing him the next time.

## Why Rescuing Never Works

Think back to when you were growing up. You probably remember vividly the times you suffered the natural consequences of your actions. Perhaps you left a beloved doll out in the rain or neglected your schoolwork. If you learned your lesson, it was probably only because your parents refused to rescue you. They did not bring your doll inside, nor did they badger your teacher into giving you a better grade. As you held your ruined Barbie doll or suffered through summer school, you may have been angry or felt your parents somehow let you down. Chances are, however, you did your best to avoid making mistakes like those again.

Most of us would agree that parents who misguidedly protect their children by shielding them from the consequences of unacceptable behavior stunt their ability to become mature, responsible adults. If you find yourself always rescuing your mate, you've met one of these grown-up children. You may be in love with one now. When you continually rescue your mate, you ensure that he will never have the reason, the resources, or the will to change his behavior or solve his own problems. Why should he?

Rebecca came into my office ready to divorce her husband, Paul. But she was having difficulty telling him she wanted to leave. When I asked her why, she answered, "What will he do?"

Rebecca and Paul had started out in a traditional relationship, in which he provided the income and she took care of the house and their twins. From the day she met Paul, she had always felt sorry for him. He had suffered a terrible childhood of abuse. Rebecca tried to rescue him emotionally, by feeling sorry for him and excusing his antisocial, withdrawn, and pouty behavior.

Once Rebecca returned to work, Paul became ambivalent about his job, claiming he wanted to start his own business. Now, five years later, he had only a part-time job and contributed nothing to the family's expenses. Rebecca paid all the bills, handled all the child care, cooked, cleaned—did everything. She demanded nothing from Paul and was now troubled about how to tell him she wanted out.

"I'm hoping he'll decide to leave since we're no longer sleeping together, and he has to know that something's wrong," she said one day.

"Why on earth would he leave?" I asked. "He has it made! He won't leave until you stop being nice to him and cut him off financially. And even then, I'm not sure he'll go. You need to throw him out."

Rebecca burst into tears, "What will he do?" she cried. Even as Rebecca was trying to leave Paul, she couldn't stop rescuing him.

We like to believe that people kick their addictions, trade bad habits for good ones, and behave responsibly because they want to be good people. Human nature, however, tells us otherwise. We are notorious for seeking the path of least resistance, the easy way out. Changing takes a lot of work, and most of us will not change until we have exhausted all the resources that "saved" us until now. Besides, the rescuer is in the controlling role, and the one needing to be rescued is in the dependent one. Dependents do not believe they even have the power to change their own lives, and they will attempt change only as a last resort.

Suffering negative consequences is by far the strongest motivator. That's why people who suffer from alcoholism, drug addiction, eating disorders, and other chronic addictive behaviors rarely overcome their problems until they hit bottom. The appealing yet vague prospect of living a clean, sober, or healthy life is less inspiring than the pain of waking up in your vomit, spending a night in jail, or having a doctor tell you that your diet and cigarette smoking caused your heart attack. For most people, these devastating events really have to occur—sometimes several times—before they feel compelled to clean up their act. Every time you step in and make a rescue, you move your mate one step further from becoming mature and independent enough to ever be there for you.

## Why It's So Easy to Rescue Someone We Love

We might intellectually disagree when someone tells us we should sacrifice everything for him, but when he says, "I just need your help this one last time, and then everything will be great for us, honey," as he professes his love, it's hard to say no. In fact, we feel like a heel if we don't help. When we equate loving with rescuing, we lose sight of what we need and the true purpose of our relationship.

### Rescuing Makes Us Feel Noble

Our society applauds and rewards people who help others; it says we are noble and morally right to help people who are down and out. Our deeds are even more commendable if we make some personal sacrifice in the process. What most of us fail to grasp is that in personal relationships, where balance is so crucial, different values apply. Continually making sacrifices for your mate produces resentment and anger and very often kills love. There's nothing noble or right about that.

When we are overly invested in the idea that giving is *always* good, noble, right, commendable, virtuous, and so on, we overlook what we're giving up. As a result, we forget or rationalize or talk ourselves out of expressing how resentful, angry, exhausted, broke, nervous, and demeaned we feel. Isn't being a good person a higher goal than being happy, rested, financially secure, and confident? It really isn't, but we believe it is. Women are especially susceptible to these beliefs, in part because domestic sainthood has long been the only consolation prize for the real sacrifices we make. When you begin to see sainthood and nobility as the Cracker Jack prizes they really are and appreciate the good stuff you traded them for, the inequity of this bargain becomes very clear.

### We Believe Rescuing Deserves Reward

If someone rescued you, you would be eternally grateful. Or so you think. As the one doing the rescuing, you understand and appreciate what you did and how much it cost you. If, however, you were the one being rescued, you probably would have little or no appreciation for what your rescuer did for you, because the person taking usually feels entitled. This is how someone who is rescued often sees it: *I'm a person who needs help, not the one who gives it. And someday, if I ever get ahead, of course I'll help. But who could expect me, in my situation, to help anybody? After all, I'm the one with the problems. She helps me because she loves me, and I know she won't ever ask me to do anything I don't want to. If I promise to do something and I don't come through, she doesn't get mad because she knows that's just the way I am. I appreciate her help, but I also resent it because sometimes she acts like she's better than I am. But I know she really loves me because she's still with me even though I bring nothing to the relationship. I must be doing something right.* It sounds kind of cold and calculating, doesn't it?

If you and your mate have an equal relationship, you can assume that he would respond to being helped much the way you would: with appreciation, respect, and reciprocation. This would not be chronic rescuing, however, because he would be giving something back. If, however, you continually rescue your mate, it's certain that he does not see these things the same way you do. If he did, you wouldn't be rescuing him *on a regular basis.* You cannot expect justice and fairness from someone who does not share your values *and* who benefits from the inequality. If you do, you will always be disappointed.

### Rescuing Gives Us Control over Others

When you rescue your mate, you gain control over him because he becomes obligated to you—and he knows it and resents it. As long as you keep rescuing him, you can keep him quiet about some of your own bad behavior by reminding him of your helpfulness and making him feel guilty enough about the money you lent him, or whatever, that he wouldn't consider confronting you on any issue.

One reason rescuers often continue giving is that they never come out and demand reciprocation. Instead, they expect to be repaid indirectly. For example, if you give your mate money, you may think he won't leave you. Or if you give him advice about how to run his life, you will expect him to follow it. If, however, he doesn't repay the money or do what you've told him to do, you probably will not issue any ultimatums or make any direct demands. Still, you and he both know that he owes you, and so the balance of power shifts to your corner.

The condescending attitude that comes with rescuing is greatly underestimated. When you rescue him, you are essentially telling him that you are better than he is and that he is incapable of handling things himself. Rescuers also derive power from this subtle form of intimidation and one-upsmanship, but be forewarned: Even grateful mates eventually resent your control.

### Rescuing Distracts Us from Dealing with Our Own Lives

Years ago I tried to rescue everyone I knew. As a school counselor, I tried to save each kid; at home, I took care of my boyfriend, and in my spare time I helped my girlfriends manage their love lives. When a stress-induced colitis attack landed me in the hospital and my doctor recommended I stay for a week to undergo tests, I jumped for joy. *Finally,* I thought, *someone will have to take care of me.* (A footnote: By then, I'd spent so many years assuming I was right and rescuing everyone else that none of my friends imagined I could possibly need their help and support. As one friend put it, "You always seem to have all the answers. I figured you had everything under control. What could I do for you?") It took me years to realize that I had spent my rescuing days distracting myself with everyone else's problems instead of figuring out how to make myself happy. I think subconsciously I expected the gratitude of others to make me happy, but it didn't. In fact, I lost the job, the friends, and even the boyfriend I had tried to save.

No one has an infinite supply of time, energy, or emotions. Even the strongest of us need to replenish ourselves with the love and the attention of others. People who rescue others never get the emotional nourishment they need because they start forgetting that they have needs. Besides, givers have trouble taking; they don't know how. They also never ask for anything directly because they know they would be disappointed in their mate's response. To spare themselves that pain, they must deny their true feelings and pretend that they are emotionally self-sufficient. Sooner or later, however, their true feelings bubble to the surface. Instead of even considering the possibility that she should stop rescuing, however, a true rescuer thinks she only needs to do more rescuing so her mate will finally see how good she is and be there for her. The whole time she has ignored her own life and needs, and so has he, because she let him.

### We Are Attracted to People Who Need Us

When we see someone in trouble, it is only natural to want to help him and make things better. Helping others can provide us with opportunities for personal and even spiritual growth, and I am not suggesting that we suddenly turn our back on everyone in need. But before lending your mate a helping hand, you need to find out how and why he got into this mess, how often he has been in it before, and what he has done to try to solve the problem in the past. We should never try harder to save someone than he has tried to save himself.

If most or all of your friends and lovers seem to be living from one crisis to the next, you are probably involved in behavior that isn't healthy for you or the people you are helping. If you find yourself attracted only to people who have problems or if you think that someone who confides something bad about his life is more interesting and more deserving of your attention than someone who seems to have his life together, you need to examine what you are getting from these relationships. Someone may seem to need you, may constantly seek your advice, and may tell you repeatedly how no one else will understand or listen to or bear with or be there for him. All of this is probably true, and listening to him ramble on for hours about the same problems—which, by the way, he never seems to solve—may make you feel you've done something good and constructive, that you have really helped. But you haven't. You've just enabled the person to get attention for his bad behavior. And you are setting yourself up for a life of wondering why no one is ever there for you.

Now step back for a moment, and ask yourself whether this is really an equal relationship or one built on his need for your help. If the situation were reversed, and you suddenly needed real help—a place to stay, money, care for your ailing mother—would he be there for you? When you talk, is he as interested in you as you are in him? Do you mention your own problems? If so, what kind of response do you get? Does your mate show mild interest but change the subject? Does the conversation invariably end up being about him? If there is no real reciprocation in the conversation or in the relationship, do you automatically make excuses for why he can't offer you the same sympathy, support, and time you give him—at least not now?

It is easy to get wrapped up in other people's problems, particularly our mate's. When we cross the line between healthy involvement in a mate's life and chronic attraction to men like him because of their problems, we are choosing weak men so we can keep the relationship out of balance—in our favor. We excuse, indulge, and tolerate behavior and neglect that would be unacceptable were it not for the mitigating circumstances of his "problem."

We may be attracted to weak men because we are used to caring for a weak parent. Or we may find it so difficult to communicate our needs and confront someone when our needs are not met that it's just easier to be with someone we have no expectations of. Or we may feel unworthy and believe that our caring and our advice are really all we have to offer, that we would not know how to act in a relationship with a healthy, self-sufficient, and mature person who didn't need us. We may even think, *I know he has problems, but at least I can count on him staying because he needs me.*

## We Want to Be Understanding

We have all felt victimized at one time or another, by parents and/or by other people. We remember those times when we had—or wished we had—someone to turn to. We like to think of ourselves as compassionate and generous. In an age in which no problem is taboo, we pride ourselves on our enlightened attitudes toward people who, for example, were abused or are addicted. It is appropriate to be understanding of a mate who has suffered problems like these and to help him deal with his issues in a patient, compassionate manner. But that is not the same as letting your mate's past issues or current problems define and run your relationship. Your mate is not unique in having problems; we all have problems. The difference between someone who gets on with his life and someone whose life is perpetually in crisis is not the cards life has dealt him but how he chooses to play them.

## We May Be Co-dependent with Our Mate

In recent years, there has been a lot of talk about co-dependence, the state of being in a relationship in which one person has an addiction to a substance or a compulsion to overindulge in a behavior—such as drugs, alcohol, sex, violence, spending, eating, or generally living on the edge—and the other person protects him from the natural consequences of his behavior. If you do anything to keep an otherwise non-functional or semifunctional person's life going—call your mate's boss to make excuses when a binge keeps him home from work, pay his bills after he snorts his last paycheck, or always deal with his family so he doesn't have to—you are co-dependent. Co-dependent behavior ranges from listening as a compulsive shopper whines about his short-tempered creditors to buying an addicted person a drink.

But co-dependency goes even deeper. People who are co-dependent often believe that they are in some way helping the person who is dependent when in actuality they are helping perpetuate his destructive behavior. Co-dependents may say that they would do anything to help the addict stop drinking, drugging, spending, eating—whatever. Unfortunately, the reality is quite different. What would help the most is to back off and allow the addicted person to face the consequences of his actions, and the co-dependent has trouble doing this. Just as the addicted person has assumed a role, so has the co-dependent.

Professionals who treat alcoholics and drug addicts have observed that once someone becomes clean and sober, his loved ones are often unable to determine how to create a new role for themselves. Accustomed to dealing with an irresponsible, immature, uninvolved, or generally incapacitated person, they are confused by, and sometimes even angry with, the new sober person who has emerged. As he rewrites the terms of the relationship and begins participating, perhaps for the first time, the co-dependent partner may become so displaced that subconsciously she encourages a relapse. Or the prospect of a full recovery may so terrify the co-dependent that she almost ensures that the dependent never gets help.

As tough as it may be to love a mate who has ongoing problems, when we do, we always know who we are in the relationship, and we are always needed. Those around us who don't think we're crazy view us as saints. Because co-dependents persevere against the odds, they believe their love is somehow better than that of healthy individuals. After all, they may reason, it's easy to love a man who has it all together. But someone like poor Johnny?

As with many behaviors, co-dependence is something you may have learned at home. You may have begun playing the role of co-dependent by helping your father hide his liquor bottles, promising not to tell your father how much your mother spent on clothes, or always pretending that one or both of your parents were not drinking, gambling, drugging, or having affairs.

Co-dependence is pervasive because it looks and feels so much like love, but the belief that loving someone means helping him is very hard to overcome. For one thing, we have numerous false beliefs about loyalty, bearing a loved one's burden, and not doing anything to hurt someone you love. For another, you really don't want to believe that you can't help your mate. But the truth is that you can't, and nobody can. The person you are co-dependent with probably has problems that will not be solved by simply trying to force a change in behavior. He may need years of professional treatment and/or therapy to resolve his problems. Some practitioners believe that substance addictions and alcoholism, as well as compulsive gambling, eating disorders, and sex addiction, have biochemical aspects that no amount of confrontation or talk can conquer alone. The only way you can help your mate is by insisting that he get help, and by not enabling him to function as easily until he does.

That said, however, you have to remember that a relationship based on co-dependence is by definition out of balance. Although it may feel comfortable to you, perhaps even rewarding, until you acknowledge the role you're playing in sustaining an unhealthy relationship, there can be no hope of change. Unless you determine why you have sought out and tolerated such a relationship, you are very likely to find yourself co-dependent with the next man, and the one after him.

## The Truth About Rescuing Your Mate

No matter how much you know, how much your "helpless" partner owes you (emotionally or financially), and how truly you believe you are running the relationship, you are not really in control. You may make a lot of noise, give a lot of directions, talk a lot about which turn was the wrong turn, make the car payment, check the oil, and fill the gas tank, but ultimately you are just a backseat driver. The mate you rescue is the one at the wheel. "But that can't be," you might be saying. "He's jobless/addicted/depressed/a victim himself. How can he possibly be in control? He couldn't do anything without me." And there you're half-right: He does need someone who won't demand he reciprocate, who willingly and repeatedly puts his interests before her own, who never asks and never receives—all while she's patting herself on the back for her behavior. But that partner does not have to be you. People in co-dependent relationships find it hard to face the fact that their mate stays with them because they support his dependence. One reason co-dependent mates don't push for change is that they ask themselves what role they will have under the new regime, and they know that in many cases the answer is that they will have no role.

## How to Stop Rescuing Your Mate

### Identify and Work Through Past Issues

Rescuing is learned behavior, and most rescuers learned the behavior as children. In most cases they may have had to take care of a sick mother, younger siblings, or an alcoholic father.

At four o'clock one morning, a policeman knocked on Vicky's door. With him was her fifteen-year-old "baby" sister, Gloria, who had been picked up for breaking the town curfew—again. Vicky promised the policeman it wouldn't happen again and pleaded with Gloria to behave. Gloria cried, promised she would stay out of trouble, and told Vicky how much she loved her. The next day, Gloria ran away. A week later Vicky's latest boyfriend, Stuart, crashed her car and was arrested for driving under the influence. She took a leave of absence from work to care for him until his broken leg healed, then, a month later, handed him the keys to her new car.

When I asked her why she put up with Gloria's and Stuart's behavior, Vicky shrugged and began to cry. "You don't understand how it is for them; they have really bad problems. I have to help them because I love them. If I turned my back, what kind of sister, what kind of girlfriend would I be? I just thank God I'm strong enough to be there for them."

Vicky had felt this way most of her life. She and her older sister, Carly, were in their early teens when their parents divorced and their mother was diagnosed as having cancer. For three years, they spent every moment when they were not in school taking care of their mother and being "little mothers" to Gloria, who was then a toddler. Because they loved their mother and Gloria, they pretended they didn't care about all the things they missed: extracurricular activities at school, sleep overs at their girlfriends', and summer camp. Later in life they thought it was normal when the men in their lives depended on them to solve all their problems and never reciprocated emotionally.

Vicky and her older sister left home when they were in their late teens. Not surprisingly, both quickly fell into rescuing relationships. Men from broken homes, men with drug and alcohol problems, and men who were abused figured prominently in their lives. Both Vicky and her older sister disdained people who, in their opinion, didn't "care enough" about others to help them, and they often talked about their friends' and boyfriends' problems as if they were their own. The only time Vicky ever felt she truly belonged was when she could help. She didn't know how to have a relationship with someone who didn't need her. Vicky went through a string of boyfriends and two husbands with drug or alcohol problems. Carly avoided men with substance-abuse problems, but her boyfriends were always less ambitious than she and unable to solve their personal problems.

The turning point in Vicky's rescuing came the last time Gloria called, sobbing, to say she'd lost her job and been evicted. Vicky had been in therapy now for several months and was beginning to understand why she rescued others. Therapy had helped her finally become angry enough to want to stop. Six months before, she and Carly had warned Gloria that they would not rescue her again, and despite her anguished, heartbreaking pleas, they stuck to their promise. It wasn't easy; they spent hours talking each other out of trying to find and help their little sister and discussing how their childhood had set them up to be rescuers. When Gloria finally reentered their lives, a year later, she was clean and sober, employed, and with a responsible mate. Without her sisters enabling her, Gloria had finally grown up.

Vicky was able to stop rescuing because she realized she was not responsible for undoing the damage that had been done to Gloria and her myriad dependent ex-mates. She was freed by the knowledge that there was nothing she could have done to save her parents' marriage. And once she had her own child, she allowed herself to be angry about, and to mourn, her own lost childhood. She also recognized how much she actually had grown up needing to be rescued herself, and she realized that since she had pulled herself up by her bootstraps, anyone could. Vicky no longer had to prove that she deserved love, and she began evaluating potential mates and friends in terms of what they offered her, not vice versa.

## Know the Difference Between Rescuing and Supporting Your Mate

One of the first times I ran into Alan before we began dating, I asked him to defend me against a male friend of his who was being very critical. I was surprised and walked away when he replied, "You're a strong woman; handle it yourself!" Later I confronted him about this, and Alan (who had been in therapy and was aware of his pattern) explained, "I've rescued women all my life and am tired of it!" I replied that all I had been seeking was his support, since I had already handled the problem by confronting the offender and asking him to leave me alone. I wasn't asking Alan to handle the situation for me; I only wanted him to acknowledge to me and to his friend that he agreed with me. Whereas I was looking for direct support, Alan believed he was providing support by demonstrating his faith in my ability to handle my own problem. We were both right.

While rescuing a mate involves trying to fix his life, lending support involves being there for him, listening, showing empathy, and most of all, sending him the message that you believe he can solve the problem himself. When you love someone, you need to help him on his journey, not carry him down the road.

You can keep your relationship in balance and protect yourself against rescuing your mate by keeping a constant check on how your mate responds to your help. If despite his problem, he maintains the willingness and ability to reciprocate, he is not asking to be rescued. If he seeks advice as research for a plan of action rather than as a lazy substitute for never taking action and is able to advise you at times, you are not rescuing him. If the problem shows concrete signs of improvement or if it is really beyond his control (for example, he has lost his job due to downsizing) but he makes the appropriate adjustments to deal with it (seeks another job, takes over household responsibilities while you go to work or work more hours), you are not rescuing him.

## Don't Let Others Set You Up

Does the person you're dating expect you always to buy lunch while he squanders his money on stereo equipment? Does he ask for your help directly—say, with his rent payments or with his dealings with his family—then accuse you of trying to run his life? Or does he simply say, "I don't know what to do about . . . ," hinting that he has unmet needs you may be able to help him with? Situations like these set you up to be a rescuer. Learn to recognize requests for help and advice as invitations to rescue.

You can decline the invitation by avoiding situations that lead to rescuing. If, for example, you paid for lunch last time, let your date know in advance that you expect him to pay next time, saying, for example, "Don't forget. It's your turn to buy!" If he balks or offers some excuse for why he can't, say, "Let me know when you're ready to take me to lunch." In other situations, if your mate solicits, then resents, your advice, respond to his next litany of complaints not with "Well, honey, I guess I could . . ." but with "What do you plan to do to solve the problem?"

Don't take on the identity of a rescuer. Make sure that whatever help, advice, or support you give your mate is reciprocated regularly. It's fine to help a little, but do so with clear limitations in mind. If your mate loses his job, for instance, you may agree to lend him money, but with the understanding that it will be paid back by a certain date. In some situations, it is appropriate to assume greater responsibility. If, for example, your husband is experiencing an unusually high level of stress due to work commitments and his mother's terminal illness, you would probably expect less from him in terms of household chores and child-care duties. Discuss the situation openly, however. Then redress the balance in the relationship in other ways (hire a baby-sitter to watch the kids on Saturdays; get help with the housework), and reduce your other commitments (entertain his business associates at a restaurant instead of at home; make sure that he asks his siblings to contribute to their mother's care). Later, be sure that he reassumes his responsibilities once the crisis has passed.

## Don't Listen to Whining

As any parent can attest, whining is a kid's ultimate weapon in the war of wills. Two-year-olds know that whining gets attention, and this is one lesson from childhood few of us ever forget. Adults who whine also seek attention, and they know that if they whine long enough, eventually someone will rescue them from having to deal with their problem themselves. When we solve someone else's problems or listen to his endless whining, that person achieves the same result as the child: He doesn't have to attend to the work of running his own life.

The best way to deal with a whiner is to remember that people who whine don't necessarily have more problems or worse problems than other people do. Look around, and you'll see people who face incredible obstacles every day but don't whine about them. Instead of focusing on the problem your mate whines about, turn your attention to the problem of his whining. Stop viewing whining as an opportunity to feel good about yourself because you listen, and see it for what it usually is: a bad habit, one that you can help your mate break.

In a relationship, whining is dangerous because it sets us up to rescue our mate, and it sets him up to need to be rescued. Whining is designed to wear us down, so the more whining we listen to, the more apt we are to rescue someone. If you are involved with a whiner, think of how many times you've said, "If I have to hear about that one more time . . ." or "I can't stand listening to that anymore." Chances are you may have been driven to the point where you would do anything to make the whining go away, including solving the problem for him.

If your mate whines continually about the same problems, you need to let him know how you feel and set a firm boundary. Say, "I really care about you, but I must admit I'm getting tired of hearing you constantly complain about the same problems. I'd like to see you do something about your problems for a change. Let's make a deal: You can tell me about a problem only if you also have a plan of action for taking care of it. If you start whining again, I'll remind you by asking, 'What are you doing about it?' "

At first, he'll be hurt and think you don't care. He may even challenge you to prove that you love him or accuse you of abandoning him. To a certain extent, this is understandable. After all, by tolerating his whining in the past, you've sent him the message that it's OK with you, and now you're changing the rules.

Make him see how whining makes you feel and how you think it's hurting the relationship—for example, say, "Listening to you whine is depressing and makes me think less of you." Remind him that every moment spent whining is a moment not devoted to kissing, cuddling, laughing, or sharing. Every moment you listen to him whine is one less moment for you to share your own feelings, to feel his support and his love. After the next hour-long whine fest, you might say, "I'm sorry you're upset, and I understand that you might feel better for having talked about this problem. But frankly, I've already heard about it, and I now feel worse. We could have spent this hour having fun—making love/eating dinner/driving to the beach—and we both would have felt better for it. Let's try that next time instead." Agree on specific times and circumstances under which you can discuss possible solutions to his problems or better ways to deal with them. You might say, "We can talk about how our day went for twenty minutes before dinnertime; then I want to have fun or talk about something upbeat." Tell him what, in your view, your relationship is (a source of mutual support) and what it is not (a dumping ground for problems and issues you choose not to address); then post the NO DUMPING sign, and lock the gates.

Be honest about your feelings about how his whining is damaging the relationship. You might say, "When you bring up the same problems over and over again, I feel overwhelmed. I care about you, but the fact is I cannot solve your problems for you. I hate to see you so unhappy, but I also resent the fact that you expect me and our relationship to suffer the burden of your unhappiness while you do nothing to change the situation. If you don't know what to do, then get some professional help to figure it out." Point out what his whining is doing to the balance between you. Tell him that when he whines, he is asking you to act as his mother rather than his lover and that he gives you good reason to feel resentful and angry. When you stop listening to his whining, he will be hurt at first, but in the long term you are finally helping him break his bad habit of whining—which ultimately will help him take charge of his own life.

### Share Your Own Problems

When we give the impression that we have no problems, we attract people who will lean on us. Unless we make clear that we expect our relationships—all our relationships—to be reciprocal, we invite people to look to us to solve their problems and rescue them. You may have your life under control (especially compared with others around you), and you may feel that sharing your own problems, worries, and frustrations reflects negatively on you. You may be so repulsed by the whiners in your life that you never want to talk about your own problems. This is a mistake for two reasons: One, you are inviting people to expect, even demand, that you take care of them. Two, you are removing yourself from a position where others could support and help you. The people in your life need to see your areas of vulnerability. They need to hear your feelings, wants, and problems.

People who want to be rescued usually eliminate others in the same boat from their list of potential rescuers. They don't want to have to compete for attention. Given a choice between someone who shares her own problems and someone who seems to have none, they will choose the person who appears to have the world on a string. If you think this isn't so, test it out. The next time someone starts whining, at the first opportunity, say, "Me too." Then start telling him about your problems and watch him get bored and disappear. Don't forget to tell him what you are doing to solve your problems so you don't actually become a whiner.

For most of my adult life, I tried to rescue my mother. I would listen to her problems, tolerate her whining, and give advice (which she rarely if ever followed). The whole time, she was doing nothing to solve her problems or remove herself from her situation. One day in a phone conversation she told me, "Sometimes I just feel like killing myself." When I responded, "Sometimes I do, too, Mom," she stopped in her tracks and remarked, "Not you. You've got a great life." When I started telling her how this wasn't necessarily true, she seemed uncomfortable and suddenly had to hang up. When I changed and began to tell my mother about my own problems, she ultimately took me off the pedestal, started listening and asking about my life; and I then felt more loved and supported by her.

Karla realized that every phone conversation with her boyfriend, Tom, invariably evolved into a whining-rescuing session. She put a stop to it by beginning to answer truthfully whenever he asked, "How are you doing?" She told him about her current problem, stressing what she was doing to solve it. If he began whining, she carefully avoided offering him advice or help. After five minutes, she tried to change the subject, and when that didn't work, she simply said, "Tom, I believe that my listening to you go on and on about this is counterproductive. It isn't solving your problem, and I'm sure you can find a solution on your own." At first, Tom was taken aback, but after Karla did this several times, he began talking less about his problems and doing more to solve them. Once he even remarked, "You know, I never even thought that you might have problems, too. You seemed to have your life so under control. I'm really sorry."

## Wean the Takers

If your husband has leaned on you financially for the past three years and you're tired of it, it's very hard to just say, "No more!" You can wean him from his behavior gradually, however. Begin by telling him that you are no longer willing to be responsible for 100 percent of the family income and why. Perhaps you are working overtime to cover the bills, or you have postponed returning to school at night to complete your master's degree. Maybe you just want more time to yourself. Set small, realistic goals. He must provide, say, 15 percent of the income, or find a way to cover the groceries or his own clothing expenses at first. Regularly increase the amount you expect from him until your contributions are more equal. You can apply the same principles to correct any imbalance: in housework, child care, time spent with your respective relatives, and so on.

## Monitor Your Rescuing Behavior

Accept the fact that you have been rescuing people because doing so fulfills a need in your life. You have not suffered for others all these years simply out of the goodness of your heart. You probably derived some sense of satisfaction, self-esteem, and control from rescuing them, and this may be hard to give up. Become more aware of why you started rescuing others in the first place, and ask yourself why you continue doing it now. When someone seems to need your help, what do you feel when you decide to give it? What do you expect will come of your efforts? What really happens instead?

Before you offer to help someone, ask yourself what sacrifices you'll be making to provide the help and whether you will resent it if you get nothing back. Don't convince yourself this person will come through "this time"; make your decision based on the worst-case scenario. If you won't have the airfare to attend your best friend's wedding because you paid your boyfriend's rent (yet again), won't you resent it? If you'll be stuck at home all summer with your mother-in-law because your husband feels obligated to invite her but can't stand being around her, won't you resent it? Remember, the question is, "Will I resent it?" not, "Why am I doing it?" or "What will happen if I refuse?" or "How will he feel if I put my foot down?" If you know you would be angry and resentful, don't do it. Resentment inflicts damage on relationships that nothing can repair.

Remember, you are controlling your own behavior to change his. Be especially careful not to give unsolicited advice or offer unsolicited aid. If you want to advise your mate, ask him first, "Do you want me to tell you what I would do?" Respond only if he says yes. At the same time, however, don't continue to listen to whining or "yes, buts." If he refuses your input or tells you why it won't work and begins complaining again, say, "I gave you my idea. There's nothing else I can do to help you. I understand how you feel and I sympathize, but there's nothing for either of us to gain by simply restating the problem over and over again."

As you wean a taker, you must not only not listen to his whining, but also be on the lookout for your own feelings about losing control of him and the relationship. You may be so used to rescuing and doing for others that you're not sure what your new role should be. Begin creating one by visualizing a more equal relationship, one in which your mate nurtures and supports you. Imagine give-and-take in every aspect of your relationship. Be clear about what you want and what your new role will be. Then share that information with your mate, and sit tight. Remind yourself that changing his behavior and yours will take time and patience. Whatever you do, resist the temptation to jump back in and save him, even if it means leaving the relationship.

## A Last Word on Rescuing Your Mate

Rescuing is a controlling, condescending, ultimately self-defeating mistake. It never helps your mate or your relationship, and sooner or later whatever love you might have shared will be poisoned by mutual resentment and the fact that your own needs have been neglected. It is neither virtuous nor wise to do more for someone than he is willing to do for himself or for you. No one gets through life without hitting some rough currents and deep water. If your mate hasn't yet learned to swim, it's time he did. If he refuses or "can't," then you need to recognize his position for what it is: a choice. Before you blindly dive in next time, remember that every time he goes down, he takes you and the relationship with him. Rescuing never saves anyone. Take your energy, instead, and put it into making your own life the best it can be.

# 8

# Mistake Number Six:
# Taking Your Mate for Granted

Jack, forty-five, and Sue, thirty-eight, have been married seven years and have a four-year-old son, Elliott. Sue quit working as a newspaper reporter when the baby was born, and Jack, a police detective eligible for early retirement, took up the financial slack by teaching a couple of evening courses at a nearby college. Originally, Sue planned to stay home with Elliott until he started school, but a year ago, she was offered a position as editor of a magazine. The pay was great, and she would be able to work at home two days a week. Eager to finish fixing up their Victorian house and resume their free-spending, pre-baby lifestyle, Jack and Sue agreed that she should return to work.

Because Sue's boss warned that she might be called upon to travel on short notice and her hours could be long during deadline weeks, she and Jack hired a full-time (but not live-in) nanny, Lea. *At last,* Sue thought, *Jack can stop teaching the night courses, and we can have time together again.* But then Jack was offered the job of his dreams: the chance to teach more courses, with the understanding that when he retired, he would have an assistant professorship. Jack said yes.

For the first few months, they felt they had it made. They bought a new minivan, spent several thousand dollars on the house, and rented a summer beach house. Then, in June, Sue's boss quit suddenly, and she was pressed to assume his responsibilities "temporarily." Jack was not getting home until after nine three nights a week, and Lea agreed to work later those nights only if she could stay over in the guest room. Feeling they had no other choice, Jack and Sue reluctantly agreed.

By that fall, Jack and Sue seemed to have everything but time; they made it to the beach house only three weekends all summer. Every Saturday was a tedious blur of errands: Elliott's daddy-and-me class at Gymboree, the dry cleaner's, the car wash, the grocery store, the health food store, and whatever else. By nine o'clock, Jack and Sue were both asleep in front of the television. Sundays they attended church, then usually had dinner with Jack's mother or Sue's parents. Most Sunday nights, one of them looked after Elliott while the other finished the chores. What little conversation they did have revolved around finding Elliott's favorite toy and confirming their schedules for the upcoming week. Their long farewell morning kiss was replaced by "Don't forget to pick up Muffy from the vet on your way home from Elliott's play date Tuesday."

"I won't. And remember you promised to take my mother shopping Wednesday night."

"OK. Bye!"

"Bye!"

One day when Sue was out of town on business, Lea called in sick, leaving Jack alone with Elliott. While he was reading a fax from his office ("urgent," as usual) and running to answer the door, Sue called. "Honey, I missed my flight and can't get home until tomorrow morning. Please don't forget Elliott's play date today and don't forget I told my dad you'd help him move that furniture." Before Jack could even answer, or say I love you, Sue cut him off.

"Gotta go. Bye!" Jack hung up feeling overwhelmed and unloved. *Who does she think I am,* he asked himself, *the houseboy? What the hell happened to our marriage? Can't she at least say "please" and "thank you"?* Of course, Jack didn't even have time to think about this. Across the room, little Elliott was pounding his toy credit card into Sue's computer's floppy drive with a plastic hammer.

It is all too easy to stop appreciating what we've got, especially when it's something that comes easy to us or has been around for a long time. There's an old saying that you never miss your water until the well runs dry, and that is especially true in relationships. When we find true love, we just assume it will last forever. We may start off cherishing those qualities that make us feel most secure—his dependability, his always being there, his willingness to help—and loving him for them. If we're not careful, however, we can easily begin to regard these products of our mate's devotion, love, and caring as no more remarkable or no more apt to disappear than that old couch in the den. Not only do we all need to be loved and appreciated, but we all need to be reminded of it every single day.

If you catch yourself thinking, *Well, he knows I love him,* or *He doesn't mind spending every Saturday afternoon with my folks,* ask yourself why you believe that. Have you told him that you love him? Have you asked him whether he knows how much you do? Have you asked him whether he enjoys the obligatory time spent with your family? When we take someone for granted, we make assumptions about him. Yet if we examine those assumptions closely, we soon see that they're usually based on nothing but our opinion of how he should feel.

This is one mistake almost all of us make to one degree or another and one we should pay special attention to since it's the first step to letting passion die. In the next chapter, I will discuss how to keep your sexual relationship alive and strengthen the bonds of intimacy. Here I'm concerned with a far more common, insidious problem. Interestingly, these are

---

### Are You Taking Your Mate for Granted?

- Do you spend more time on work, the house, and the children than you spend alone with your mate?
- Do you spend nonquality time with your mate feeling either bored or stressed?
- Do you think of your mate more as family and less as the exciting, romantic person he was when you first met?
- Do you share your feelings more easily and more openly with friends, family, and strangers than with your mate?
- Do you view going home to your mate as something you have to do, not something you look forward to?
- Do you seldom make an effort to look your best when you are with your mate?
- Do you seldom play or spend spontaneous time together?
- Do you say more negative comments to your mate than warm, loving ones?
- Do you treat your mate more like a roommate than a lover?

If you answered yes to any of these questions, you're probably taking your mate for granted.

---

not so much two separate problems as they are two different stops on the same bad road. While they are related, and the first can certainly lead to a diminished sexual relationship, taking your mate for granted should be considered a serious problem in itself.

Every couple is at risk of making this mistake, although the longer two people have been together, the greater the risk. This is because once we begin to feel secure in a relationship, we feel less of a need to make that special effort, show that extra consideration, or include some gesture of affection in our jam-packed day. *After all,* we reason, *I know he loves me, and he should know that I love him.* Although that may be true, that's where the problem begins. He may know that you love him, but if you begin taking him for granted, he sure won't feel that you do.

Seven years into my relationship with Alan, I felt fairly secure. Once we became committed, he was always dependable, doing what he said he would do, never giving me reason to doubt his word. When we met after work for dinner, he always greeted me with a loving smile and gave me his full attention as I told him about my day. Unlike my other relationships with men, in this one I never really worried about him not being there for me. Then one night out of the blue, Alan phoned me later than usual and seemed to have an attitude. He was pulling away from me, and I was not sure why. After many subsequent talks, he finally let me know that he felt I had not been listening to him and I was taking him for granted. There were also some other danger signs—namely, several young women who seemed to enjoy his company a little too much. He reassured me that he was not even thinking of having an affair, but looking back, I can see that if I'd continued taking him for granted, he may have allowed one of them to do the listening I was forgetting to do.

This was not the first time I'd been accused of taking someone for granted. Once I stopped being a rescuer, I had become quite self-involved (it's common for one to go to the opposite extreme). In recent years my girlfriends had accused me of valuing my time more than theirs, of always talking about myself, and of expecting them to be available whenever I had a rare free moment. And they were right. Now I was doing this to the man I loved. Early on I had really appreciated Alan's thoughtfulness and dependability, and I let him know it. Then, as I began to get used to those qualities and feel comfortable in the relationship, I just assumed he would always be that way because that was just the way Alan was. After all, he would never stop being the responsible man I could always count on. Or so I thought. Alan's sudden change in attitude toward me made me reconsider these assumptions and stop taking him for granted. Fortunately, he was open and honest enough to let me know before it was too late.

No one has it easy these days. Most of us—men and women alike—are working harder than ever, on the job and at home. Couples with children have additional responsibilities and even less time. It's no wonder, then, that we start taking shortcuts: forgetting to say "please" and "thank you" or assuming that because he always handles certain chores, he always will. When we take our mate for granted, we often deny him the simple courtesy and consideration we extend to others. We become convinced that we know him thoroughly, so we just assume that the restaurant we choose or the time we'll be away from home attending school at night will be OK with him. After all, he never seems to complain, and he's probably not going anywhere. Even worse, we also assume that a serious relationship is like an opened bottle of champagne— destined to go flat sooner or later anyway. When we find ourselves only half-listening to him, when we spend every free moment together attending to chores, and when we let the daily grind drain all the spontaneity, joy, and kindness from our interactions, we are not only allowing our relationship to lose its sparkle, but we are also risking permanent damage.

## "There's No Time for Us"

Robert and Celeste are typical of older couples who take each other for granted. An attorney they had consulted about getting a divorce referred them to me after they changed their minds and decided to give their marriage one last try. By the time they appeared in my office, their relationship was a disaster. Robert was so depressed about it he was having suicidal thoughts, and Celeste, who had not worked in three years, felt powerless both inside and outside the home. They seemed to be different from each other in almost every way. He had a rigid work ethic and she did too, but only for him—

the husband who should provide well—not for herself. She liked to talk all the time, and he longed for peace and quiet. He longed to travel once he retired, and she refused to board an airplane. They had been passing each other in the hallway for over twenty years and finally woke up one day and asked why they had stayed with each other all this time.

There wasn't much of a bond left between them, so rebuilding the relationship would be difficult. Over the years, they had stopped trying to maintain or develop mutual interests, and each had totally gone off on his or her own. Since Robert had been in the world of business, and she had stayed home until the children started high school, they felt miles apart.

Not only had they both been taking each other for granted, but they didn't even know what quality time meant. They had let anyone and everyone come between them: their three grown kids, the grandchildren by their youngest son, and their own parents. They treated their acquaintances better than they treated each other. Neither had anything left to give himself or herself, much less the other. When I asked Robert what he would ask for if I could wave a magic wand and make his fantasy come true, he replied, "A day to myself, self-sufficient kids, for Celeste to be more independent, and for my parents to be more financially secure." And what did Celeste want? "Emotional fulfillment with my husband."

When Robert began looking at what his marriage had come to, he realized that home had become a series of power struggles over who would handle which responsibility and that his marriage to Celeste was nowhere on the list of priorities. He couldn't imagine how he and Celeste could ever fix their relationship since they'd grown so far apart. For instance, he wanted to buy a motorcycle, and she wanted to save more money for their retirement. She made it clear to him that a fifty-nine-year-old grandfather had no business tooling around on a motorcycle. Every time he shared any of his ideas with her, he felt as if she were raining on his parade. That's why he had begun to act like merely a roommate and had stopped bothering to talk to her about anything that mattered to him.

Robert and Celeste were not only taking each other for granted; they were also taking their lives for granted. Their lives had become a boring routine of obligation. Robert said, "We always spend Sundays with my family." Celeste said, "Robert always comes home straight after work." "We always" and "we never" ruled their lives, leaving little room for personal freedom, spontaneity, or adventure. No wonder Robert began longing to take off on a motorcycle and never return.

## The Many Ways in Which We Take Our Mate for Granted

Taking our mate for granted can include anything and everything from forgetting to say "I love you" at least once a day to the extreme of having an affair. This is another mistake that has its roots in false beliefs and is amply nurtured by our assumptions about how love should be.

So how do we take our mate for granted? Let me count the ways.

### We Do What Everybody Else Does

Unfortunately, we often model our own behavior on that of couples who are making the same mistake themselves. In their circle, even Jack and Sue know only other two-income couples. The last time Jack broached the subject of married life with his best buddy, they both concluded that their decidedly unromantic, hectic, debt-ridden lifestyle was inevitable. And though Robert and Celeste socialize with several other couples, they rarely all go out together. Celeste and the wife go shopping while Robert and the husband take in a game of golf. The concept of quality time with their husbands is sometimes discussed by Celeste and Sue, but both laugh and agree it's a mere fantasy.

If you recognize taking your mate for granted as a mistake you are making, be especially careful not to justify it on the grounds that most other couples you know behave much the same way. True, you and your mate are not the only ones squandering a sunny summer afternoon cruising the aisles of Home Depot, you're not the only ones whose romance seems to be on automatic pilot, and you're not the only ones at the cocktail party ignoring your mate. But the fact that you are not alone does not diminish the risks you take by following this course.

Many of the behaviors and attitudes we believe are typical and normal between mates—interrupting, nagging, acting more like roommates than lovers—are symptomatic of taking someone for granted. They are behaviors we would barely tolerate from, or engage in with, strangers, yet we see nothing wrong with them when we direct them at our mate. *After all, everyone else seems to be doing it,* you may think. Perhaps, but if you want a relationship that's healthier and stronger than those around you, you have to learn to recognize how you take your mate for granted and stop doing it.

## *We Stop Giving Our Mate Top Priority*

When you first met, you had very definite goals in mind: to nurture love, to build a relationship, possibly to marry, to begin a family, and to create a home. All these desires were fueled by love—not buddy love or friend love but the romantic, all-consuming, passionate love you and your mate shared then. That love is what brought you together and made your dreams come true. Jack and Sue are typical of many couples who have become so focused on what their love has created—the children, the dream house, and so on—that they devote time to everything but the love that made it all possible. Whether you do this because you feel strapped for time or because you truly believe that your love can take care of itself, the result is sadly predictable: Romantic love wanes.

We all have responsibilities, but we also have choices. We may be engrossed in our career or consumed by the need to have a picture-perfect house. We may feel that chauffeuring the children to a dozen activities every weekend is time well spent or that maintaining a high profile at the club or in the PTA is extremely important. Women are already preprogrammed to do too much; that's probably why we find ourselves feeling exhausted and overcommitted. Although we may derive great personal satisfaction from our activities, we must recognize the trade-offs involved. When we habitually choose to spend our valuable time and energy on people and things other than our mate, we all but guarantee that he and our relationship will suffer.

### We Stop Showing Consideration

In love, little things mean a lot. A heartfelt thank you, an unexpected kiss or hug, an offer to let your mate sleep late on Saturday while you walk the dog for a change—these are all ways in which you show your mate you are thinking of him and that he matters. In a balanced, healthy relationship, these gestures are reciprocated freely. When you are out among others, you and your mate should treat each other with the same courtesy you show anyone else. That means listening when he speaks (not butting in to correct him or to add some detail he forgot) and inviting him to join your conversations with others. You may assume you know how he feels about things and make decisions—about the kids, the weekend, the holidays, the house—on his behalf without consulting him. Sometimes this is unavoidable, and you two may have agreed that certain things fall under your jurisdiction or perhaps he really does not care where the two of you go on Saturday night. The mistake here is assuming that you know without asking.

## *We Act Disrespectfully Toward Our Mate and Toward the Relationship*

Once you get comfortable with a mate, you stop viewing the relationship as a growing, ever-changing entity and start regarding it as a done deal, something you've brought home and must learn to live with. You often treat your mate less respectfully, more like the way you treat family. You may begin to see him less as an individual and more as a reflection or an extension of yourself, much as your parents regard you. Suddenly, his every mistake and shortcoming makes you look bad, so you feel justified in nagging and criticizing him to bring him around to your way of thinking and acting. When he speaks, you're nodding your head but glancing up at the television, hearing only half of what he says and not offering much in the way of a response. Instead of exploring and trying to correct problems in the relationship, you write them off to his being just the way he is. You assume that he will never change, and that's your excuse for not making any effort, either. You start to forget that unlike the family you each came from, you two are together today by choice.

No matter how much we may claim to love our family, the fact is that family members often endure one another's worst behavior. And if we're honest with ourselves, we know that we would be mortified if friends or business associates ever witnessed some of the things we have said and done in the presence of family. Yes, families can be close, but they can also be dismissive, demeaning, manipulative, and unpleasant, secure in the knowledge that family members rarely demand better treatment and that family will always be family. When we start thinking of our mate as just family, he becomes anything but the romantic object of our desire and compassion. Sometimes we do this because we are modeling behavior we have seen in our homes or in other relationships. Other times it is because we have allowed resentment to build; rather than approach him directly and air our real grievances fairly, we launch indirect attacks, sniping about this and that. But it doesn't matter why you lose respect, romantic love cannot stay alive without it.

## We Spend an Increasing Amount of Nonquality Time Together

Most of us are pressed for time, and so we try to do things with our mate whenever possible. The problem is that love did not take hold simply because the two of you were together; it flourished because of the quality of time you spent together: where you went, what you did, how you felt. When I speak of quality time versus nonquality time, I'm not suggesting that every romantic encounter can take place only on a white-sand tropical beach. (In fact, many couples make the mistake of waiting for such perfect opportunities, which of course come too late.) What I'm saying is that spending too much of the wrong kind of time together can be as detrimental as spending no time together at all. Nonquality time is spent in situations that discourage meaningful, intimate communication and/or crowd out more enjoyable activities. Being together while you're plopped on the couch not talking or cuddling but, watching whatever happens to be on TV, taking care of the kids, or dealing with other work- and family-related obligations will never produce the intimate togetherness you experience when you're doing things both of you truly enjoy.

Wives whose newly retired husbands are underfoot, mates who run a business with their spouse, and couples who insist they do everything together—from paying the bills to folding the laundry—are all suffering from a surfeit of nonquality time. So are couples who allow themselves to get locked in to a routine—such as spending every Sunday with extended family even if something more interesting comes up or designating every Saturday errand day. Familiarity between two individuals may not breed contempt exactly, but it creates a cozy incubator for the boredom and petty grievances that turn the man of your dreams into someone you just cannot stand. When mates spend too much boring, mundane time together, they suffer a kind of guilt by association. If most of your time together is unstimulating and boring, you not only become bored with him, but also risk your mate's viewing you as unstimulating and boring. And you may well be, since the more time you spend with him doing nothing, the less you have for yourself, which means your personality loses its sparkle.

To avoid spending too much nonquality time together, see whether your plans for next weekend would pass the date test. You're probably not the only couple who spent the last sunny weekend shopping for your mate's mother's birthday present, Junior's school supplies, or that new circular saw. But ask yourself, *Is this what memories are made of? Are these places I would have wanted to go with him when we were dating?*

While there are certain errands and responsibilities you must see to, and some of them do require both of you, there may well be others you can either scratch or do separately. Jack and Sue, for example, with their busy schedules, couldn't create more time, but they did learn to allocate what they had more efficiently. In exchange for a half day off during the week, their nanny, Lea watched Elliott every Saturday night so Jack and Sue could start dating again. Sue and Jack each promised to do two regular errands, like taking the clothes to the dry cleaner's, during the week so that Saturdays could be more relaxing. Then they let their parents know that they were welcome to watch Elliott after church (more time together for Sue and Jack) but that they wouldn't be staying for dinner every Sunday.

### We Form Emotional Attachments Outside the Relationship

Ask yourself, *When something really good or really bad happens in my life, whom do I call first and whom do I talk to most about it?* If it's not your mate, then you are more emotionally attached to someone else than you are to him. You may say, *Yes, but it's my mother/my sister/my best friend, Mary. Isn't that OK?* In my office, when women confront their husband about not being emotionally available to them, the first thing most husbands say is "If you weren't on the phone to your mother/sister/friend so much, maybe I would be there for you."

Women often rely on the emotional support of other females in their life to the exclusion of their mate, sometimes without even realizing it. Others believe it's the only choice they have. When it seems difficult talking to their mate about their life, these women often give up and go back to their female support systems instead of resolving the problem with him.

I realize it's often much easier to share our deepest feelings with someone other than our mate. Even in the best of relationships, there exists the real possibility, no matter how small, that expressing our true self will drive our mate away. Our fear of judgment or rejection often inhibits us from expressing ourselves to him. When we stop expressing ourselves, however, we loosen the bond, and our need for emotional intimacy goes unmet. We feel that something is missing. That's why people often end up having affairs when they really didn't want to: They needed someone to talk to.

I addressed this issue in Chapter 4, "Expecting Your Mate to Read Your Mind," and I will repeat it because it is so important. Whenever you bring others into your relationship—whether it's by divulging secrets or having an affair—you are committing emotional infidelity. It's especially damaging to talk about your mate in a way that will cast him in a poor light. Betraying his confidence and degrading the relationship in the eyes of others damages the emotional bond, even if your mate never knows you've done it. In letting off steam by talking to everyone but your mate, you are more apt to go along with the status quo and never address problems with the only person who can really help you change them: your mate. For example, bored Celeste was able to tolerate her disappointment in Robert and in their relationship because every time she felt angry, she called up her sister, Betty, and ranted for an hour about how distant he was.

Sometimes we rationalize these conversations on the grounds that we are protecting him. In fact, however, we are damaging our bond since the negative feelings we have—as well as the reason why we have them and the problems they create—won't simply disappear. And if you haven't told him what the issue is, he can't fix it.

## Why We Take Our Mate for Granted

### It's Easier to Fall in Love Than to Stay in Love

When we first fall in love, everything is so easy. Once we grow comfortable in the relationship and pass important milestones, we begin forgetting how we got there in the first place. We decide we need a raise, so we put in extra hours at work for the next six months. We feel tired and overwhelmed, so we try to avoid unpleasantness at home by keeping our feelings to ourselves. As Jack drives home after a long day, the last thing he wants to deal with is the argument he knows he'll get if he asks Sue to cut back on her hours at the magazine. Robert let it go, but kept thinking that someday he would tell Celeste how he felt, but by the time he did, it was too late. She was ready for a divorce and it didn't make any difference.

We keep thinking we can have that long talk, that romantic evening, that special time together later or some other time. But that time never seems to come. Between work, the house, the kids, the in-laws—it's always something. The relationship has withstood everything until now; we're sure—or at least we hope—it will weather this onslaught of neglect as well. It will be there when we get around to it, whenever that will be.

People who believe this set themselves up for cruel and bitter disappointment. Yes, hard, stressful times do sometimes make relationships grow stronger, but only when there is a strong bond and the two of you are talking, sharing, and supporting each other through those times. Your mate needs and deserves attention, love, and respect, especially when he is stressed; we all do. Finding a way to meet our basic emotional needs is simply human nature. A neglected mate will begin withholding love or will find someone else to appreciate him, or both. Every relationship produces misunderstandings, and at one time or another we have all felt misunderstood, unloved, unappreciated, or hurt by our mate. When we feel stressed—because of him or because of other things—and we don't make the time to discuss our feelings honestly, we carry them inside until we feel so resentful that we find it impossible to be vulnerable and open to love. Often we use our resentment to justify our own bad behavior, and the relationship suffers even more.

### We're No Longer in Love with Him

Maybe you feel you were never really in love with your mate. Maybe you married young or on impulse or out of desperation and fear of loneliness. Maybe the better you got to know him, the more you realized that you two were not right for each other. Perhaps you have simply grown and changed so much that it would be impossible to continue having an honest, meaningful relationship. Or you still love him but in a nonromantic, family way, for example, as the father of your children or as your family's provider.

Once you have fallen out of love, it is very hard to maintain a bond that involves honesty and integrity. If you try to pretend you love him when you don't, you risk hurting him and losing your own sense of self and passion for life. If you find yourself feeling that you are not really in love, you need to face the problem and discuss it with your partner. Seldom do couples manage to rekindle their love once it's dead. If you know the love is gone, staying and taking him for granted isn't good for either of you.

### We Forget to Be His Lover

In traditional relationships, it's common for partners to assume certain roles: he, the breadwinner; she, the mother and homemaker. Today, even with both partners working, we may still subscribe to certain roles and divisions of labor. If you do assume several roles, there is nothing wrong with wearing several hats—as long as you remember to change them frequently. Unfortunately, few of us have role models for couples who work, are devoted to their children, and maintain their romantic spark. Our daily responsibilities so overwhelm us that it seems easier just to stick with one role and wear the same hat all day. You must remember that regardless of who you are to your children, your friends, your boss, your clients, or your family, you have to protect your identity as your mate's romantic partner.

Many couples stay married for years while they are distracted by work, children, building a home, and nurturing a family. It is not until they wake up one day to discover the children grown and on their own that they see how their family life overshadowed and smothered their romantic bond. Once their role as full-time mother or full-time father has come to an end, they find themselves actors without a script, as Robert and Celeste were after twenty years of focusing on "the family." They don't know what to say, what to do, or even how to feel. They have grown and changed so much that the romantic roles they played years—maybe even decades—ago just don't fit. Unfortunately, most couples fall back into the security of their family roles and so stay together for the sake of the children or the grandchildren or because they fear they would have no identity if the core of the family disintegrated in divorce. They may use work, the family, or hobbies to bind them together—for the wrong reasons. Such couples believe that their marriage can never be what it was, and they cannot imagine creating a new romantic bond based on who they are today. Don't let your relationship evolve to that point; remember to continue in the role of lover every day.

### We Become Too Self-Involved

One of the reasons I fell into the habit of taking Alan for granted is that I became too self-involved. My career was booming, so I threw myself into it. I traveled more, I talked about myself more, I spent more time totally focused on my career goals. Alan made it easy for me to do this by listening, giving support, and talking less and less about himself. At the time, he was not happy at work and was contemplating a job change, and it was hard for him to interrupt me to say, "I'm happy for you. Now let me tell you what a miserable day I had." When Alan stopped talking about himself and did not demand that I listen to him, I misinterpreted this to mean that he was fine and wanted to hear more about me. I also failed to see that talking so much about myself was sending him the message that I was not interested in him or his problems. Nothing could have been further from the truth, but caught up in my own exciting life and sitting across from my seemingly rapt audience of one, I lost sight of what sharing is really about. Instead of using communication as a means of sharing my world with Alan and his with me, I inflated my coups and my triumphs until anything Alan might have said about his life was bound to be overshadowed.

It is very easy to get caught up in your own life and to develop tunnel vision, seeing only your own problems and achievements. The heart of a good relationship is communication, but, as I said earlier, not all communication is created equal. Talking to hear yourself talk is not making the most of your time. It almost does not matter whether you are complaining or crowing, the problem is that as long as you're talking, you're not listening. Furthermore, you may not feel particularly compelled to listen to your mate when the subject is something you don't fully understand, like his job or his interest in sports. One couple I know, Ed and Sonia, both worked in book publishing when they met. For their first few years together, Sonia enjoyed listening to Ed talk about his day at the office. But since last year, when he set up shop as a consultant to companies using the Internet, she has said he bores her. The minute Ed starts talking cyberspace, Sonia drifts off. Ed has started to notice this and has pulled away emotionally. I suggested that the next time Ed wanted to share his stories about work with her, Sonia should not focus on his anecdotes but should ask him to tell her how he feels about them. From there, she can steer the conversation to his pleasure, his enthusiasm, and his success. As long as Sonia is not enabling Ed's whining or letting him talk about, rather than solve, his problems, she needs to be a part of his life by listening and letting him know that she is proud of him and happy for him.

One of the strongest bonds between partners comes from the sense that it's you and me against the world, that we are equals in every sense, full participants in our own life as well as in the life of the relationship. When we become overly absorbed in our own life, we command a disproportionate share of attention. When we fail to reciprocate by listening to our mate and offering our support, we relegate him to the role of bystander rather than participant. It is difficult, if not impossible, to maintain a sense of equality and shared interest in a relationship when one partner is constantly behaving as if her individual concerns were more important and more deserving of attention than her mate's.

## How to Stop Taking Your Mate for Granted

### *Recognize When and How You Take Him for Granted*

Old habits can be hard to break, especially if they are ones you see repeated around you. If you find that you take your mate for granted in any of the ways I've discussed, admit it. Resist the temptation to defend yourself with such rationalizations as these:

- "But we've always done it that way."
- "He's never complained about . . . before."
- "I know that if it really bothered him, he would have said something by now, and he hasn't."
- "I just assumed that he didn't mind entertaining my friends every weekend/listening to me talk for hours about my work/always doing the grocery shopping."
- "He knows I love him and appreciate him; I don't have to say it."

There is no excuse for taking your mate for granted. The sooner you accept that, the sooner you can change your behavior and avoid the resentment being taken for granted inevitably creates. Think of several of your more recent conversations. Ask yourself, *Did I really give him my full attention when he was speaking? Did I listen to him as much as or as well as he listened to me? Did I interrupt or correct him? Did I minimize his problems or not take them as seriously as he did?*

Think about times when you were alone together and times when you were out among others. Think about how you spend your time. Do you routinely accept invitations and make commitments on his behalf without asking him first? Is your schedule filled with more things you have to do than things you want to do? When you are out together, what kinds of activities are you engaged in—dating or drudgery? As you look at your date book, is quality time with your mate marked in red ink or just penciled in, pending other demands and subject to change?

## Vow to Keep Love Alive

If you suspect you have been taking your mate for granted, put yourself to the test. If you find that you have to make a conscious effort to show your appreciation and respect, chances are you've been taking him for granted.

As I have said throughout this book, our behavior often reflects beliefs and attitudes that we accepted without question, from our parents, previous lovers, and peers. Based on your observations, it may seem normal to let love and romance die as two people grow old together, but it's healthy to keep love alive. Don't you want the two of you to be the little old couple who grew deeper in love the older they got?

## Deepen the Bond Between You

The bond between two people in love develops over time, and likewise, it may be lost over time. To regain the bond, you and your mate will have some catching up to do. Think about the last time the two of you felt really close—before you began to take each other for granted. It may have been before your first child arrived, before his or your big promotion, or before the move to the new house. Without blaming yourself or your mate, talk about what happened and how you both contributed to the change in your relationship. Step through the years since then, discussing major incidents and pinpointing those periods when you each felt the best and the worst about the relationship. Discuss what you both could have done differently. Reprioritize. Together the two of you may decide not to buy that new, bigger house and instead spend some of the money on intimate vacations. Maybe

### How to Keep Love Alive

1. *Be affectionate.* Touch, kiss, hug, and cuddle regularly without always leading to sex.
2. *View and protect your relationship as a third party.* Set aside quality time for it, just as you would for a friend or a child.
3. *Renegotiate the roles in your relationship.* Design your own relationship instead of blindly copying society's standards.
4. *Reexamine those things you and your mate* always *and* never *do.* Be more discriminating in how you spend your time together.
5. *Show your appreciation every day.* Tell him that you love him and why. Instead of just "I love you," try "I love your beautiful smile/your great buns/the way you handle the kids."
6. *Cherish your memories, and create new ones today that you can cherish tomorrow.* Remind your mate of the good times.
7. *Play together.* Start a pillow fight, break out the Monopoly game, or put on the songs you listened to when you were first dating.
8. *Establish small but important quality-of-life rules around the house, such as:*
   - no shouting from room to room
   - no interrupting
   - no television or unnecessary phone calls during dinner or after eleven o'clock at night
   - limit shop talk to an hour or so an evening
   - no nonemergency business calls at home.

you'll wait until your relationship is back on track before having another child.

Negotiate between individual goals for the future and goals for the relationship. Don't hold back any thoughts or feelings. Make a promise that neither of you will take the other or the relationship for granted again. Decide on a key phrase you both will use if you sense it may be happening,

### Five Great Intimacy Builders

1. *Talk about your relationship.* Check in regularly to see how your mate is feeling toward you. Is he harboring any resentment, hurt, or disappointment? Hear him out, and share your own feelings. Let him know that doing this makes you feel closer to him.
2. *Reminisce about the good times you have shared.* Continually remind each other of the incidents that have made the two of you close.
3. *Share events of your life, past and present, with your mate.* Talk about how you felt when your first puppy died, when your teacher called on you in class and you didn't know the answer, the time you caught a previous lover cheating on you, and so on. Ask him to do the same.
4. *Check in with each other during the day when possible.* Ask him how his day is going, and tell him about yours.
5. *Be spontaneous, and break out of your daily routine when you can.* Stay up late, go for a midnight stroll, meet him for a drink after work, or make a surprise meal.

such as "Don't forget, honey, it's you and me against the world."

Every day brings a noisy parade of people and things clamoring for your attention. While you may feel overwhelmed by these demands, the fact is you do pick and choose who and what will engage your time, your energy, and your affection. You can choose to make your mate and your relationship a priority, if you really want to. With forethought, energy, and creativity, you can develop and protect your relationship *and* make it better than ever.

# 9

## Mistake Number Seven:
## Letting Passion Die

One of the saddest things I hear anyone in my office say is "I love my mate; I'm just not 'in love' with him/her anymore." In a mere dozen or so words, I hear pain, regret, sadness, resignation, and hopelessness. Of all the Seven Dumbest Mistakes, letting passion die is the most insidious because it is usually the product of things we neglected, forgot, or never learned how to do. Because this mistake involves sex, we are probably less comfortable discussing it with anyone, including a mate, than we are discussing any other issue in the relationship. Passion dies with a whimper, not a scream, and most couples don't notice the damage until a crisis sets off an alarm. Typically, that crisis is a possible or consummated affair, and by then it's sometimes too late to salvage the relationship.

Couples whose love thrived in the glow of their sexual passion almost never recognize how they got to where they are now. It all happened so gradually, they often say, if they noticed it at all. They might say they just stopped having sex.

Usually, they assume this is to some degree normal and that even if it is not, there is little or nothing they can do about it. There's the job, the kids, the pressure—you know. Or as one woman said, "I've accepted the fact that it can never be the way it used to be." It's as if they're watching their private, golden paradise grow smaller as the tide pulls them farther out to sea.

Mandy and David are in their early thirties, have been married only three years, and are still very much in love. They are affectionate and often kiss, touch, and cuddle, but they seldom have sex.

Mandy teaches school full-time, and David runs a chain of restaurants as well as other ventures, working an average of sixty hours a week. When the subject comes up, he complains to Mandy that he's just too tired for sex. Though her day is equally exhausting, she still wants to have a sexual relationship with David, and she wonders whether something is wrong. David claims that he is still attracted to her, and he tells her that he's overworked, that it's temporary, and as soon as the next job is complete, he'll have more energy and everything will be back to normal.

Only later in therapy—prompted by Mandy's almost beginning an affair—did the couple open up and share their real feelings. Mandy told David that she felt very lonely because he was hardly ever home, and when he was, he was too tired to do anything with her. He responded by saying that he loved her, then added that he felt Mandy wasn't being supportive of his career. She, on the other hand, was hurt that David did not respect her profession and said that he behaved like a parent when he told her she should stop teaching and become an entrepreneur like him. David said that he was so tired of her crying every time he talked to her about this that he had just stopped communicating with her altogether, which led to his no longer having sexual feelings for her.

Like most couples, David and Mandy had to deal with sexual problems and hang-ups from their past and work on other aspects of their relationship as well. What is most important for you to understand, however, is that the mistake of letting passion die begins with a breakdown in communication. Failure to communicate is the first silent snowball that eventually triggers the avalanche. No matter what other problems couples unearth as they work through their loss of passion, their inability to communicate sets them on a course from which they may never find their way back, even when they want to desperately.

Because both Alan and I had made the mistake of damaging bonds by letting passion die in previous relationships, we are conscientious about protecting our love today. At different times, both Alan and I have done things that could have endangered the bond, but we caught ourselves in time and stopped. As I worked on this book, for example, there were times when I practically ignored him. Whenever one of us felt a distance begin to creep between us, we spoke up immediately and directly, often joking and using our code phrase: No distance between us. Most important, however, we dealt with the problem right then—not next week, or when my project was done, or when I felt a little better. Even though Alan said that he understood why I was not as available as I had been, I did not let myself believe that was all there was to it. I made sure we immediately spent some quality time together.

It sounds like it was such a little thing, but that's the secret of preserving the sexual bond: The so-called little things mean a lot. In therapy, couples who have let passion seep out of their relationship eventually reveal that the wall between them rose slowly, almost imperceptibly, as one small hurt was matched by another and another until one day they simply could not reach around the wall. When we contemplate or hear of someone we know having an affair, we tend to think that the affair is the problem. In fact, what led to the affair usually was not one big explosion but the cumulative effect of dozens or hundreds of little annoyances, resentments, and grievances that grew in silence.

If you have learned only one thing from this book, it should be that you must take personal responsibility for the course and quality of your relationship. This is especially true when it comes to protecting the integrity of your intimate bond. Beyond your bedroom door lies a host of forces—personal sexual hang-ups, societal assumptions about what's normal, an increasingly hectic lifestyle, to name only a few—that can destroy the most precious part of your love if you do not learn to recognize the early warning signs and work to put your relationship back on track. It is sometimes possible to rekindle the passion, but I must warn you, of all the Seven Dumbest Mistakes, this is the one that most often proves fatal. Ironically, it's also the one that could be most easily prevented if only we knew what to look for and how to fix it.

## The False Beliefs That Make Us Drop Our Guard

Which of the following statements are true for you?

- I think it's normal to be less interested in having sex with your mate after you've been together for a while.
- I believe our sex life will improve once we have more time/we go on that great vacation/the kids move out, things will get back to normal.
- I would like our love life to be wild and passionate again, but I've accepted the fact that it probably won't be.
- Before, the bottle chilling in the fridge had a cork, not a nipple; the tub was a love nest, not an aquatic preschool learning center. Is it any wonder the romance has died?
- Since I've gained weight/turned thirty [or forty or fifty]/had children, I just don't feel like my old sexy self.

If any of these statements ring true for you or even sound vaguely reasonable, stop! You are in danger of letting the passion fade from your relationship. I can almost hear you saying, "Maybe, but he hasn't said anything about it. He feels as tired/pressured/overwhelmed as I do. Is this really a problem?" Yes, because by accepting these attitudes and developments as normal, you are buying into false beliefs that undermine an active and fulfilling sex life.

When we were younger and our relationship was new, sex—hot, wild, and breathtaking—came so easily we probably never gave it much thought. Those sparks, that magic—it just happened because he was the one. If we are honest with ourselves, though, we can see that even when it seemed simple, we did in fact put a lot of effort into making our love life—and ourselves—sparkle. Our mate became the focus of our attention and our affection. We talked to him, we flirted, we complimented, we teased. We thought about what we would say and how we would say it, what we would wear, what we would do. Most important, we considered how he would feel, what he would like, and how we could make sure he knew how much we cared.

Yes, as people spend more time together and come to know each other truly, the relationship does change. The mystery and excitement that come from a relationship being brand new do fade. But in a healthy, strong relationship, the relationship grows, and so do its partners. As couples grow and change together, mystery and excitement may come and go but the ever-deepening intimacy and trust can create a deeper sexual bond.

## Why Sex Is So Important

In a romantic relationship, sex is the crucial ingredient that distinguishes the two people who are "in love" from those who love each other like family. In cooking, it would be the difference between instant pudding and a divine mousse, grape juice and champagne, scrambled eggs and a soufflé. Because good sex requires the ultimate in vulnerability, trust, honest expression, and total emotional commitment, there is nothing in the context of a relationship that can replace it. It's fine to admire your husband because he's a good provider, to be proud of the lifestyle you share, or to be totally involved with the fine children you two have raised. It's wonderful that you two are best friends, full partners in everything, and have a marriage all your friends envy. These are all worthy goals and hallmarks of a stable, healthy relationship, but none of them will bond you two as intensely and as uniquely as having good sex together will. When you neglect the sexual aspects of your relationship, you not only weaken the bond from within but also remove a part of yourself from the relationship and close the door to the private sanctuary only the two of you shared. And although we make assumptions about this being normal, we don't really accept that it is. If we did, no one would be having affairs.

## Why We Let the Sexual Bond Unravel

### We Stop Thinking of Ourselves as Sexy

Recently I heard someone remark, "In America, sex is an obsession. Elsewhere in the world, it's a fact of life." Our puritanical heritage haunts us at every turn, and despite the countless books, magazine articles, and talk shows we are notoriously inhibited when it comes to discussing sex. We are bombarded by sexual imagery, yet we would be shocked to see an ad for condoms or birth control devices on television. We believe we are sophisticated about sex because it seems to be everywhere, but if we look carefully, we see that the sexual message we get is limited. The prevailing cultural ideal of what is sexy revolves around the minority of people who are young, rich, fit, beautiful, and single. Although intellectually we dismiss these images, they take their toll, and we find ourselves fearing we somehow just don't measure up. At the same time, we can't imagine certain types of people (like parents) or those over a certain age or who aren't model-thin even having sex. When we find ourselves now fitting into one of these categories, we question our right to remain sexually expressive and whether or not we are even considered sexually attractive by others.

Throughout this book, I have discussed how much we learned about relationships from what we saw modeled at home. Unless you were fortunate to have parents who were affectionate, romantic, and flirtatious in your presence, you probably still cannot even conceive of them having had any kind of romantic relationship, and especially not a sexual one. As a result, you often unthinkingly assume that good mothers/wives and good fathers/husbands don't do it.

## We Lack Knowledge About Sex

Once two people in a relationship settle down, they usually embark on a series of dramatic life changes. They may begin to focus more intensely on progressing in their careers, buying a home, accumulating wealth, and having children. These are all positive developments, but they are also time-consuming and stressful. Because the courtship phase is now officially over, these couples may see their sexual relationship diminish yet feel no compulsion to improve matters by learning more about sex. If both are sexually naïve, they may find the subject hard to deal with since any suggestion that their sex life might be improved assumes there is something wrong with one or both of them. If one partner is more curious and adventurous about sex, the other may feel intimidated, pressured, or insulted by attempts to try something new.

As we grow older, we expect our horizons to broaden, and we naturally become more discerning and more sophisticated in our interests and tastes. Over the years, you've probably developed new hobbies or a deeper level of interest in old ones. Odds are the cuisine, décor, movies, books, clothing, ideas, and activities you prefer today are in your judgment better, more interesting, more stimulating, more exciting, or more satisfying to you than those you liked before. Yet we seldom think of sex in these terms. Most of us have spent more time considering and experimenting with new hairstyles or living room furnishings than we have with our sex life. No matter how much we may enjoy sex and love our mate, the same choreography will eventually become less exciting, if not downright boring. Some couples become so entrenched in a predictable sexual routine that baking a cake or working late at the office really is more interesting.

## *There May Be Physical Problems*

Most people are not aware of the ways in which certain health conditions, medical treatments, and medications can adversely affect their sex life. Many times the problem develops so gradually that couples often attribute it to anything *but* a physical condition. If either you or your mate is experiencing diminished sexual desire or physical problems (impotence, discomfort during sex, inability to achieve orgasm), talk to your doctor, and consider the following possible causes.

*Side effects of prescription and over-the-counter medicines.* Medications commonly prescribed for many conditions— among them, high blood pressure, anxiety, depression, nasal congestion, and allergies—can hinder sexual performance. Certain kinds of antidepressants, such as Prozac, can reduce or eliminate the ability to achieve an orgasm.

*Decreasing, low, or erratic hormone levels.* As men and women age, they produce smaller quantities of sex hormones. In men, a drop in testosterone can result in diminished sexual

desire, an inability to maintain an erection, fatigue, and depression. In women, the decrease in the supply of estrogen
(which begins around age thirty) can result in a range of problems, including diminished sexual desire and discomfort during sex.

If you are premenopausal or have entered menopause,
you may want to discuss hormone replacement therapy
(HRT) or alternatives to it with your doctor. There are dozens
of HRT regimens available—even some that combine estrogen with testosterone (which can also increase sex drive in
women). Finding the one that is right for you and improves
your sex life may require some trial and error, since every
woman responds to HRT differently.

*Other physical conditions.* If you or your mate has suffered
a serious or chronic health problem, it may have changed your
way of viewing yourself as a physical, sexual person. For example, men who have survived heart attacks and their mates
often fear that vigorous sex will set off another heart attack.
Women who have had a hysterectomy or surgery for breast
cancer may feel that they are no longer desirable. To resolve
these issues, you might need to consult a physician or some
professional trained in this area of counseling.

*Fertility issues.* When women are having or have had difficulty conceiving, they and their mate often begin to view sex
as a choreographed, goal-oriented activity. After months or
years of watching the calendar and timing intercourse, one or
both may feel that sex has lost, and may never regain, its romantic aura. When women have failed to conceive or have suffered a miscarriage, the couple may come to view sex as a
saddening reminder of their loss. If you have had such an experience, I strongly urge you to seek professional counseling
to deal with the loss.

*Birth control.* It is difficult to stay totally focused on the
joy of sex if in the back of your mind you're wondering
whether your birth control method is comfortable, conve-

nient, or foolproof. Your body has probably changed, too. Perhaps you've begun to think that ten years on the pill is enough, or you no longer want to deal with the inconvenience of a diaphragm or condoms. You may also have changed some of your attitudes about birth control or an unwanted pregnancy. Perhaps you have completed your family and want to consider a permanent birth control method, such as vasectomy or tubal ligation. Whatever it is, find the solution that works for you and your mate today.

### We Don't Talk About Sex

It's difficult for most people to talk frankly about sex because, well, it's about sex. We think we shouldn't have to talk to our mate about what we want sexually. After all, we didn't have to in the beginning. What we fail to recognize is that as people grow and change, what they want and need sexually can change, too. What we couldn't get enough of ten years ago is now just plain irritating, or the leisurely massage that made us impatient when we saw him only once a week is now the stuff of our daydreams.

Even if we are free of hang-ups about discussing sex, when we discuss it within the context of a relationship, we must also deal with a range of potentially threatening emotions: love, rejection, failure, guilt. We fear that if we open a discussion about what we want or how we might improve things, our mate will reject us or make us shoulder the blame. At one time or another, most of us have been criticized for our sexual performance, and we never really forget the pain of that experience. We worry now that our mate will think that the problem is us.

But we must talk about sex for it to improve. Pick a time when you and your mate are alone and undistracted. Using the Four Steps to Healthy Communication, tell him how you feel. Explain why you believe your sexual relationship is suffering and how important it is for you to change it. Ask him to tell you how he feels and to commit himself to working with you on solving the problem.

## We Build Resentment Instead of Resolving Issues

When we choose not to confront our mate about our anger, hurt, and disappointment, the emotions do not magically disappear. As you have seen throughout this book, people who think they've hidden their true feelings rarely fool their mate. Just as most rivers eventually run to the sea, resentment eventually finds expression, and often it is in the sexual aspect of the relationship. Every negative thought you had about your mate, every insult you felt he directed at you, and every unresolved disappointment is a wall between the two of you. Until that wall comes down, you will not feel the attraction, admiration, and good feelings you need to feel to desire him sexually. Besides, since we view sex as a precious gift we bestow, it serves almost too well as a punishment when we withhold it. Besides, we know neither of us is likely to confront the other about a topic that we can barely discuss comfortably or that makes us feel so vulnerable.

## We Lose Our Sparkle, and/or Our Mate Loses His

In our rush to merge our individual selves into a couple, we often lose our individuality. Believing that couples must agree on everything, we may have smoothed all the rough edges and thrown out the pieces that didn't quite fit our picture of the happy couple. My client Jeanne gave up the offbeat artist friends her husband, Arnie, wasn't crazy about; in turn, she talked him into selling his beloved Harley-Davidson hog because it scared her. Though they made these sacrifices willingly, Jeanne and Arnie lost a part of their identity and their self-esteem along with the things they gave up. The problem may be compounded if what drew you to your mate initially were the pieces that seemed to clash, those unusual facets of his personality that made him exciting and intriguing (like the fact that Arnie was a tax attorney who sang in a rock and roll band on weekends). If you ask Jeanne and Arnie, both would probably say that the other isn't as interesting as when they first met.

In trying to change our mate to make him more compatible with us, we often dim his sparkle without even knowing we're doing it. Early on, you may have admired his desire to climb the ladder at work; today you ask him to work fewer hours so he can help you more with child care. Or you loved to see his boyish joy as he played shortstop with his softball team; now, at your urging, he's given up the league to do those things husbands are supposed to do. He was proud of your community activism then; today he considers it time spent away from the family. Or he used to compliment you on your athletic figure and smart wardrobe; today he complains when you spend too much time working out and shopping, and he worries about whom you talk to when you're away from the house.

Without realizing it, couples often trade their dating lifestyle for one less conducive to romance. Jeanne has tossed out the silk teddies from her boudoir trousseau and has begun wearing oversize T-shirts to bed and, she rejects the idea of making dates for sex as "contrived" and "artificial." Arnie crawls into bed after a night at the gym reeking of Ben-Gay. Their bedroom, once their private sanctuary, is now a multipurpose family room, where diapers get changed, sick kids get cuddled, and Jeanne and Arnie's work papers litter the floor. Now that they have important responsibilities, they can't imagine letting the answering machine pick up the phone or taking the day off just to stay in bed. As I warned them both, you cannot dismiss or ignore sex and expect to feel sexually attractive to each other.

## *We Carry Sexual Baggage*

Maybe you were exposed to sexual dysfunction in your family. You may have been sexually abused as a child and/or come from a home where sex was considered dirty and people who enjoyed it were believed to be bad. As an adult, you may have experienced mild or severe abuse when lovers, spouses, or other men sexually harassed or intimidated you or even assaulted and/or raped you.

If you have such experiences in your past and you have not already confronted and worked through the effects they had on you, it is imperative that you work now to resolve them. This may involve consulting a therapist who specializes in sexual abuse. For those who were sexually abused as children, the fact is that the experience always affects the present relationship in some way. The former victims may turn off to sex completely or even become sexually promiscuous. Certain activities or positions may cause flashbacks that stir up—even subconsciously—painful, upsetting memories.

In your adult life, you—like most of us—may harbor your share of painful sexually related memories: the lover who would not make love to you unless he was drunk or high; the one who criticized your body, your technique, your desires; the one who was the best you ever had but didn't remember your name when you ran into him a week later. It is important to remind yourself that people are often cruel for reasons that have nothing to do with you. I don't believe I'm male bashing when I say that some men are extremely crude and insensitive when it comes to sex because they've learned that such behavior is part of being a man. Remind yourself of how different both your mate and your current relationship are from those you've had before. Also remind yourself that you are older today and wiser and probably better in bed, too. My client Danielle, for instance, was tormented for twenty years by an ex-lover's criticism of her sexual performance. One day she was musing about how goofy seventeen-year-old boys are when it hit her: *He* was seventeen then. With that, the validity of his opinion and its power to hurt her vanished.

Sometimes that hurt can make us chase sexual rejection, meaning you want sex only from those you can't get it from. If this is true for you, you will need to discuss this problem with your mate, letting him know that the more he wants you, the more you are turned off. Meanwhile, you need to work through those rejection issues from the past.

Whatever you do, however you have to do it, refuse to carry any guilt or blame for earlier sexual abuse or confusion. And most important, protect your current sexual relationship from damage you suffered in your past. If you have a supportive mate, consider sharing relevant information with your mate. If he is receptive and understanding, involve him in helping you work through your sexual problems.

## The Affair

We tend to think of an affair as the result of one partner's losing interest in the other or seeking to have his needs met outside the relationship. We view an affair as a cause rather than an effect, of a dying relationship. We hear people say, "They got a divorce because he had an affair." No one mentions how dead the relationship was before the indiscretion. People do often consider affairs when they feel rejected, unloved, or misunderstood by their mate. There are mates who have affairs because they and their partner have stopped having sex. Yet people also seek affairs for reasons beyond what's happening in their relationship; they may be too emotionally immature to remain monogamous, or they may feel this is the only way to deal with a midlife crisis or some other source of stress. And there are couples in which one mate's infidelity so damages the sexual bond that there's no turning back, and the other feels justified in seeking an affair as well.

## *Your Affair*

The desire to have an affair is very common. Thinking about having an affair or fantasizing about what it might be like does not make you a bad person. In fact, a little fantasizing is healthy. When you find yourself entertaining such thoughts, ask yourself what you would prize in a new lover that your mate is not providing. Is it romance, spontaneity, more time together, openness, or emotional support? Have you told your mate that you miss those things and would like to nurture your relationship, to bring it back to health? Have you two honestly tried your best to address these issues and resolve them? If you have not, you may need to review the Four Steps to Healthy Communication (pages 80–81) and "How to Fight Fair" (pages 100–101) in Chapter 4, "Expecting Your Mate to Read Your Mind," and/or "Learn to Respect Your Differences, and Compromise Creatively" (page 147) in Chapter 6, "Thinking You Are Always Right." Your mate may surprise you and become the lover you're looking for.

If, however, you just can't put the idea of an affair out of your mind, and you believe you can justify it because

- you think your mate doesn't love you—
- you no longer feel close to your mate—
- you want revenge for something he has done or said to you—
- you have met someone who is attractive and you're bored and think it might be exciting—

Stop! These are all signs that your relationship is already in serious trouble. Under these circumstances, an affair would probably deal the fatal blow. If you have even the smallest inclination to try to save your relationship, forget the affair for now, and start to work on finding out if you can salvage what you have.

No matter how it happens or when or why, an affair is always a bad idea because it sets the stage for remorse, guilt, and the possible end to the relationship you have. Affairs rarely if ever wake up negligent partners and cause them to shape up. But if you feel stirred by the possibility of an affair, regard it as a blinking red light on the alarm panel of your heart. It's telling you that something isn't right. Heed the warning, examine your relationship, and make sure nothing's been neglected and everything is secure. Always remember that couples who manage to survive an affair usually do so in spite of the transgression, not because of it. If you really do believe that your mate no longer loves you and that there is no hope of reconciliation, then show your soon-to-be-ex and yourself the minimum of respect: Leave the relationship before you begin the affair.

An affair is an ever-present threat because it can happen so easily. You're sharing things with someone that you've never shared with anyone before. He's patient and understanding of your needs in a way your mate never seems to be. The next thing you know, you're making love. He takes his time with you in bed and makes you feel like the most beautiful woman on earth. He's gentle, he's caring, he's perfect. You can hardly believe such a man really exists outside soap operas and romance novels.

This man does not exist in the real world, and neither does the perfect, complication-free affair. It is dangerously naïve to go into an affair thinking it will be only a sexual fling. At the other end of the spectrum, people who expect an affair to evolve into something more meaningful fail to realize that this person they have fallen in love with—someone who either betrayed his current mate or encouraged his new flame to betray hers—will probably not change his behavior. If he cheated to be with you, odds are he will cheat on you. Statistics show that most people who have affairs eventually choose to remain with their current mate. Now, in

## Nine Steps to Heading Off an Affair—
## with Savvy and Class

1. Admit to yourself that you are attracted to the new man, and then ask yourself why. Figure out what is really happening, both with him and with you and your mate.
2. Resist the temptation to tell the new man or anyone else about problems in your relationship until you have shared them with your mate first and given him a chance to respond.
3. Don't act on the attraction until you've made an honest attempt to resolve issues with your mate. Set boundaries with yourself regarding the new man, such as *I won't stay late and talk to him. I will be polite but not flirtatious. I will decline his invitations to meet alone, and I will let him know he is not to touch me at all.*
4. Confront the new man about his flirting or even the mutual attraction, but state your boundaries clearly. For instance, tell him that you are in a committed relationship and that you want him to respect you by backing off now while you work on your relationship with your mate. Often discussing the attraction while setting a firm boundary dissipates the sexual tension.
5. Avoid the new man while you and your mate work on the relationship.
6. Keep reminding yourself that the affair you're daydreaming about, considering, or even planning is a fantasy. The new man's mystery and allure derive largely from the fact that you don't really know him. Force yourself to look at him more realistically. Concentrate on his faults, realize there's a lot you don't know about him. Try thinking of him the way you would think of the other woman if your mate were having an affair.
7. Tell your mate that someone is coming on to you and admit that it does feel good to be flattered, paid attention to, and wooed. Let your mate know that you have not acted on your impulses and that you really don't want to but that you do feel some temptation. Ask him

to help you avoid having an affair by working on the relationship.

8. Tell your mate that the things the new man is saying and doing are things you would rather your mate did for you. Tell him what your needs are and ask him to meet them. If he has pulled away, ask him why. Listen carefully to him. Try to work things out. Give him—and yourself—a chance to change and get the passion back.

9. Be prepared to give your mate an ultimatum. If he makes light of your concerns or doesn't respond, let him know there will be a consequence. Make clear that while you prefer to fix this relationship, you cannot do it alone. Warn him that you will not stay in a sexless, passion-less relationship. Let him know that if he continues to behave as he has been behaving, you plan to end the relationship.

The value of these Nine Steps to Heading Off an Affair is twofold. First, they give you the time, the motivation, and the tools you need to correct and preserve the relationship you have. Second, if your relationship is not salvageable, these steps enable you to leave a hopeless relationship without guilt and with your self-esteem and integrity intact. You can move on to your next relationship knowing that even though this one did not work out, you made your exit from the old relationship and entrance into the new one with integrity.

addition to facing the old problems that have led to the affair, you and your mate have the added complication of the affair itself and the issues it raises (trust, honesty, and so on). You also run the risk that your mate may never forgive or truly forget. Besides, in order to begin or continue the affair, you probably had to behave dishonestly or dishonorably with your mate, and this adds to your guilt and loss of personal integrity.

---

### Seven Signs That Your Mate Might Be Cheating

1. He is suddenly taking a new interest in his appearance.
2. He has developed a new circle of friends and acquaintances that you are not invited to join.
3. He has changed sexually: He's either too tired for sex or likes to be turned on in new ways.
4. He is emotionally shut down with you to the point where he no longer shares or even fights with you anymore.
5. He is experiencing a midlife crisis; his personality has undergone a change, and he's suddenly interested in new ideas, places, and things.
6. He can't seem to stand being home for very long and no longer expresses pride or interest in what goes on there.
7. He suddenly adopts a guilty or disinterested attitude of "Buy what you want, do what you want. I really don't care."

---

## His Affair

Some women just seem to know; others are all but hit over the head with the evidence yet continue to see nothing. How will you know if your mate is having an affair?

Before you confront your mate, think through what the affair means to you in terms of your values. Most people who have never had a mate cheat on them automatically assume that this "ultimate betrayal" would be unforgivable and would mark the end of the relationship, no questions asked. In fact, however, some people at least make an attempt to repair the relationship. Some couples even emerge stronger. Think realistically, and be honest. Is this something you feel you can never forgive? Is it something you want to try to work through?

Resist the temptation to act in ways that are not respectful of your mate and make you question your own sanity. Do not, for example, go through his wallet and briefcase, try to listen in on his phone calls, or become obsessed with catching him in lies. These behaviors will only exacerbate your anger, and it won't change the situation. You need to keep a clear head.

## What to Do If You Suspect He's Having an Affair

- Don't deny it or keep your head in the sand. Don't make excuses or fish around for alternative explanations for his behavior.
- Speak up and tell your mate what you suspect and why. Talk about it. Be vulnerable. Ask your mate whether he still loves you. If he says he does, ask him to stop the affair and work on the relationship. If he says he doesn't know, remind him of more loving times you two have had, and ask him to work with you to get the love back.
- Make it easy for your mate to tell you the truth. Say, "I know you don't want to tell me the truth. And if you are cheating, I cannot pretend that the truth won't hurt. But if you'll just be honest with me, we may be able to work it out. If you are cheating, however, and you choose to lie about it, you leave me no choice but to make plans to leave you."
- Give an ultimatum. Tell your mate he must either decide to stop the affair and work on your relationship or get out now—no ifs, ands, or buts.
- Hold your mate accountable for telling you what he was feeling about you when the affair happened and why. If he can't, insist on counseling.
- Get a commitment to emotional honesty. Make him promise he'll tell you when he's feeling negative toward you or unloved by you so the two of you can help prevent this from happening again.

Your goal is to make the best decision for yourself and the relationship, not to punish your mate.

Assuming your mate comes clean and agrees to work through the relationship with you, honor your part of the commitment to save your relationship. Set aside time for romance, but don't chase him. Be vulnerable, but keep your pride. Don't whine, beg, or act desperate. Don't let your entire future and your happiness hinge on whether or not he honors his commitment. Let a part of you assume he won't and prepare for the worst. Get your own life on track. Make yourself happy by pursuing interests, seeing friends, and doing those things you did before that made you the vital, exciting person he fell in love with—and that others could, too.

## How to Keep the Passion Burning, Now and Forever

### Remain a Vital, Interested, and Interesting Woman

You cannot turn back the hands of time and be exactly who you were when the two of you first met. But you can commit yourself to taking responsibility for keeping yourself and your life vibrant, interesting, and exciting. When we do things to make ourselves happy—including everything from pursuing hobbies to masturbating when he's not available or interested—we don't resent our mate for failing to make us happy.

Admit that you have allowed work, the kids, the house, the world, to come between you and your mate. Vow to steal back some private time for the two of you. When you feel you must choose between spending an afternoon doing something around the house or sneaking out for a quiet, romantic picnic, vow to be "bad." After all, what's the worst thing that could happen? Or as you might prefer to think of it, the best?

To feel and be sexually attractive, you must think of sexual attractiveness as a full-time state of mind, not just an attitude you put on in bed, then toss back into the closet.

## How to Cultivate Sex Appeal . . . Even out of Bed

1. Determine your most special or unique feature, and play it up. Choose clothes that show off your figure, jewelry that accents your hands or your face, shoes that give you that walk, and makeup and/or hair color—even if it's subtle—that gives you that extra sparkle.
2. Practice walking with confidence and pride: shoulders back, chest out, eyes straight ahead. Look as if you know where you're going and how to get there. If you don't feel it, fake it until you do.
3. When you're with friends, show that you're glad to see them. Laugh and have a good time. It's a turn-on.
4. Take care of yourself. Whether your style is a natural, well-groomed look or something more elaborate and sophisticated, always look your best. It tells everyone, "I care about myself."
5. Don't let having a cold, an outbreak of blemishes, or a few extra pounds diminish your confidence or your sexual power.
6. Always be yourself. When you're talking to your mate, be as real, honest, direct, and expressive as you would be with your same-sex friends.
7. Cultivate a good sense of humor. Learn to loosen up and laugh at yourself and at life. Humor is a turn-on because it keeps life's problems in perspective.

Remember, you and your mate were sexually attracted to each other long before the first kiss or that first special night. You were turned on by the total person, by how he treated others as well as by how he treated you and how he felt about himself. Hot lingerie, silk sheets, and a new set of handcuffs may work wonders, but they can never disguise low self-esteem, depression, or dissatisfaction. To quote an old Jefferson Airplane song, "You're only pretty as you feel inside." No props or costumes can change how you feel about yourself inside, whereas feeling good about yourself can give you a glow he won't resist.

## *Communicate with Your Partner, Especially About Sex*

Throughout this book, I've stressed the importance of communicating with your mate about everything. If you can nip your resentment over how he treats you or how he behaves outside the bedroom, you will have gone a long way toward heading off sexual problems. But sometimes we must communicate with our mate directly about sex.

It's hard to talk about sex because we worry that we will hurt our mate or he will say something that will hurt us. Once we truly believe that the words left unspoken are the most dangerous of all, however, we'll feel motivated to take this risk. It's best to talk about your sex life together before or after sex, not during, especially if there's a problem. Use the Four Steps to Healthy Communication to bring up concerns. Invite your mate to let you know what turns him on and what doesn't, whether he thinks you two are having sex often enough or too often, why he may feel he is losing interest or thinks you're more exciting than ever. Don't just ask what; ask why. This is another area in which you don't always have to agree; try to compromise creatively. He wants more sex than you're interested in? Try pleasuring him sometimes even if you don't particularly feel like being aroused. (But don't be surprised if your mood changes.)

While you are having sex, compliment your partner with words, sounds, or gestures. If you feel like letting him know that you don't enjoy something he's doing, save it for later. Instead, suggest something else he might do to turn you on even more. Alluding to jokes, movies, or past experiences are a good way to let him know that you'd prefer a certain position or type of foreplay.

## *Change Your Attitude Toward Sex*

For most of us, there are things about sex that make us uptight or turn us off. You probably learned most of them as you were growing up, possibly from your mother, who perhaps didn't like sex, or from your father, who may have wanted you to remain a virgin, or from religious leaders, who may have taught you that sex is bad. Unless you want to have the same kind of sex life these people probably had (or didn't have), you need to examine your negative attitudes and consider changing them.

We all have a right to our differences, and you may not really want to change how you feel about everything. Even so, it's a good idea to review periodically what you like and don't like, what you refuse to do and what you might consider trying at least once. Maybe you hate oral sex because past lovers pressured you to engage in it. Now your mate, who is tender and loving, would like it, but you've just refused. Try to look at it differently, and understand that oral sex in this relationship can have a positive, loving meaning.

Ask your mate directly whether there is anything he's ever thought about trying. If appropriate, tell him that you'd like to be more open-minded about sex. Just be sure that you know what your options are and how you really feel about new modes of sexual expression. Don't allow anyone to force you to try something that really bothers you or goes against your values. You might begin your exploration by reading a book on the subject. Sometimes couples find just talking about these things can be a turn-on.

### Learn to Focus on Sex

Reawaken your sexual consciousness. Keep sex on your mind. Begin thinking of yourself as a sexual person again: Pamper yourself sensually and/or sexually as you bathe; carry yourself with sexual pride; savor the look, the feel, the scent of your body (and his). Take a negative thought you have about sex ("I'm too tired at night"), and turn it into a positive one ("but what a great sleep I'll have after an orgasm"). Read books that turn you on, perhaps trashy, steamy novels or more literary-minded porn, like the works of Anaïs Nin. Whether you're fantasizing about your mate or about Batman, fantasies can work wonders for your sex life. Remember, the brain is the most powerful erogenous zone. Many couples report that fantasies really do improve their sex lives.

---

### How to Control Your Own Orgasms

1. Experiment with your body through masturbation until you are able to bring yourself to orgasm. Many women are able to do this by using their hands, while others prefer to use a vibrator.
2. Practice Kegel exercises. Aside from the numerous health benefits of strengthening the PC (pubococcygeal) muscle (the one you use to stop the flow of urine), this activity increases sensation and makes it easier to reach orgasm.
3. For the best orgasms, be on top. Having control of the rhythm and the angle of penetration can help you get the precise stimulation you need.
4. Let go, relax, and be there. Clear your mind of everything else except your body and how his feels inside yours.
5. Tune in to his orgasm. Try to sense his progression. To hold him back until you're ready, take control, and break the rhythm and/or slow down the motion.
6. Recall the sensation of the orgasms you have had through masturbation. Have him touch you in the same way, touch yourself, or use a vibrator to re-create the feeling as you pick the movement back up. Some women can bring on an orgasm simply by recalling an earlier one.
7. Once you're able to have an orgasm with your mate, hold back a bit. You can heighten sexual intensity by hovering at the brink of orgasm. Increase and decrease your level of arousal several times before surrendering to what will probably be the best orgasm you've ever had.

---

## *Rediscover Your Mate*

Slow down, and go back a little. Think of courting and seducing him all over again. The next time you kiss, pretend it's the first time. When you feel yourself or your mate start to go on automatic pilot, stop. Whisper something endearing or dirty, pull him down onto the floor, suggest you move to the bathtub or to another room of the house. With his permission, treat him like a total sex object one night, your master the next. Create scenarios, like doctor-nurse, teacher-student, and other roles that turn the two of you on.

## *Control Your Sexual Pleasure*

Many women today still complain that they can't have orgasms, yet when I ask such women whether they can have orgasms on their own, they often admit they've never tried. They are still dependent on their mate to bring them to the point of orgasm—even though they are not able to tell him how to do it.

If you have never had an orgasm, it is time to learn how to have one through masturbation. And if you can have orgasms by masturbating, but not by having sex with your mate, it's time to learn how to control your timing, your body, and his body parts to take control of your own orgasms.

## A Last Word on Letting Passion Die

Never forget that passion involves intense emotions. Wake up, be vital, be sexual, and make things happen with your mate. By becoming more sexually exciting yourself, by controlling your own orgasms, and by opening yourself to new sexual activities, you may find a sexy person you really like—yourself!

# Epilogue

The rich, rewarding love life we have all dreamed of really can be yours, and you deserve to have it. For years—like you, perhaps—I thought a great relationship was something other people had or something that didn't exist at all. If these women really had one, I reasoned, they must have been luckier than me or more lovable and less needy. And years of disappointing experience taught me that men were just too much trouble, maybe even more than they were worth. As I wrote earlier, I had all but given up on ever finding my own great love when I met Alan.

As I've said before, Alan and I have personally made most of the Seven Dumbest Mistakes, either in this relationship or in our previous ones. We were both rescuers of others when we met, we have at times both expected the other to read our minds, and we have both taken the other for granted and almost let the passion die. Fortunately, we became aware of the mistakes we were making, discussed our problems and worked through them. The warm, intimate, exciting, and loving relationship we have today did not evolve because we are smarter than anyone else or because we were just "right" for each other. The only thing we knew for sure when we first met—and something you should never forget—is that relationships weaken and die not because people are "bad" or because relationships are naturally fraught with problems, but because people don't see the mistakes they are making.

Relationships really aren't as difficult as we believe they are if you try to stop making the Seven Dumbest Relationship Mistakes by following these rules:

1. Protect your personal identity.
2. Don't chase.
3. Communicate feelings and desires directly to your mate.
4. Work through your emotional issues of the past.
5. Keep love and respect alive.
6. When your mate won't cooperate with you, withdraw and tell him why.
7. Set boundaries to change your mate's bad behavior.
8. Be a partner, not a parent.
9. Stay sexually active.
10. Take charge of your own life, not his.

A good relationship is a gift from God; it's one of life's great pleasures. However, it is a living, growing entity that must be nurtured and protected if you expect it to survive the challenges and changes ahead. When your relationship achieves balance, when you both freely compromise and commit yourselves to emotional honesty, the bond only becomes stronger. Problems can be doors to greater intimacy instead of walls between you. Open expression and vulnerability are shows of strength, not weakness. And asking for and expecting to get what you want is healthy, not selfish.

It sounds simple, and it is. Yes, men and women do have their differences, and relationships can be difficult. But we are not, as some believe, representatives of two inherently incompatible species, and relationships need not be synonymous with trouble. Each of us—men and women alike—needs love, support, and respect, and we sense, correctly, that a healthy romantic relationship can provide them in a way nothing else can. If there is one main secret of having a great relationship, it is this: You are responsible for taking control of your own life. You have the power to shape a relationship into the hot, intimate, enduring love you want if you simply understand how to stop making these mistakes.

When you choose not to write your own rules for your relationship, you are stuck trying to create the love of your future with the stuff of the past—both your personal past and the unenlightened history of male-female relationships. If you believe the relationships you grew up around or the ones you see today are good enough for you, then you don't have to worry. With enough neglect, your relationship will eventually prove unfulfilling, boring, and painful, too. If, however, you want something better (and I'll say it again: You deserve it!), throw off the false beliefs that encumber your relationship and threaten your love. If you do this, you will go a long way toward avoiding the Seven Dumbest Mistakes.

As you look around, remind yourself that what is considered normal is not always healthy. Have the courage to go against the grain in taking charge of your own life and your relationship to make them different. Make new rules that reflect who you and your mate are, not what others expect you to be. You are special, and so is your love.

Couples who make any of the Seven Dumbest Mistakes are like two pastry chefs standing at a mixing bowl trying to make one great cake out of two bad recipes. Without realizing it, they toss in ingredients that are incompatible (like abuse and love, secretiveness and intimacy), poisonous (like resentment or punishment), or unpalatable (dishonesty or controlling and dependent behavior). Instead of starting from scratch, each chef follows a different recipe. When the cake falls flat, the frosting tastes salty, and the filling is sour, each automatically assumes that the other did something wrong. They never question the recipe.

In contrast, couples who build and maintain happy, fulfilling relationships don't follow rules or recipes—they write their own. Their cake probably won't suit everyone else, and it may take them several tries to finally get it just right. They will probably be back in the kitchen many times changing the recipe to keep it fresh and interesting. But they know that's what it takes to nurture and protect something as precious as a healthy, stable, and supportive relationship. They eat their cake and have it, too, again and again and again.

## ABOUT THE AUTHOR

CAROLYN N. BUSHONG, L.P.C., is a psychotherapist in private practice who specializes in relationship and sex issues. She has a master's degree in counseling and a bachelor's degree in education. She appears regularly on national TV talk shows and is host of her own radio show. She is the author of *Loving Him Without Losing You* (Continuum 1991; Putnam/Berkley 1993) and is quoted regularly as an expert on relationships by *Cosmopolitan, Glamour,* and *New Woman* magazines. She maintains a successful psychotherapy practice in Denver, Colorado. She has helped men and women on and off the air now for more than twenty years.

Carolyn Bushong also conducts psychotherapy by phone for those who are interested in her techniques. For further information, call (303) 333-1888.

# Learn how to deal with anxiety, jealousy, and depression in romance—and get the love you deserve with

## IF THIS IS LOVE, WHY DO I FEEL SO INSECURE?

Carl G. Hindy, Ph.D.
J. Conrad Schwarz, Ph.D.
Archie Brodsky

---

It doesn't have to hurt to be in love, yet for many otherwise accomplished and confident people, romantic involvement means anxiety, insecurity, and pain. The result of the largest and most comprehensive study on this subject ever conducted, *If This Is Love, Why Do I Feel So Insecure?* unearths the causes, effects, and cures for obsessive romantic attachments—and how they prevent romantic fulfillment.

Filled with true-life stories and dramatic case histories, this provocative and authoritative sourcebook will set you on a path of greater self-understanding—and increase the possibilities of finding an enduring love.

---

"Through intriguing anecdotes, well-explained psychological methodology, and clear charts, this comprehensive book offers solace, and new paths leading out of romantic cul-de-sacs."
—KIRKUS REVIEWS

Available in bookstores everywhere.
Published by Fawcett Books.
The Random House Publishing Group
www.ballantinebooks.com